Sensational Salads

Sensational Salads

by Barbara Scott-Goodman

photographs by Judd Pilossof

Stewart Tabori & Chang   New York

Published in 2005 by
Stewart, Tabori & Chang
115 West 18th Street
New York, NY 10011
www.abramsbooks.com

Library of Congress Cataloging-in-Publication Data is on File

ISBN: 1-58479-418-6

Art Direction and Design: Barbara Scott-Goodman
Food Styling: Liz Duffy

The text of this book was composed in Gill Sans.

Printed in Thailand

10 9 8 7 6 5 4 3 2

Stewart, Tabori & Chang is a subsidiary of

LA MARTINIÈRE
GROUPE

dedication

To the memories of two great women who influenced my life, Julia Child, whose passion for great food and writing always inspired me, and my mother, a good cook who always made me eat my salad.

acknowledgments

My thanks and gratitude go to the people at STC: Leslie Stoker, for making this book happen; Debora Yost, for her suggestions and editing skills; and Jean Rogers, my copy editor, for her patience and attention to detail.

To Judd Pilossof for his beautiful photography, his keen eye, and his good nature. To Liz Duffy, for her exquisite food styling and her laughter.

To Angela Miller, my agent, for her support.

To my friends and family who always willingly sampled and commented on my dishes. And, as always, to Lester, Zan, and Isabelle, just for being there.

introduction

I love to make salads for a variety of reasons. They are healthful, easy to prepare, and, of course, delicious. Whether I serve a salad as an appetizer, entrée, or side dish, it is always an important and integral part of the meal, adding flavor, texture, and beauty. Making a salad can be a simple preparation using whatever is on hand, or it can be a big impressive production. Ingredients can be a simple but artful composition of greens and handmade vinaigrette, or they can lean toward the exotic like duck breast, bay scallops, or fresh figs. The possibilities for creating sensational salads are endless.

I realize that all experienced cooks know that they are only as good as their ingredients. That is why I let what is best and freshest at the market or farmstand dictate what kind of salad I will prepare. Until recently, salads were kind of a culinary afterthought—not the flavorful mix of greens and other inventive ingredients that come to mind when I consider salads today. I keep rediscovering the pleasures of earthy flavors found in fresh seasonal produce.

Because fresh greens, top-quality vegetables, and luscious fruits as well as beans, grains, pasta, and rice are widely available throughout the year, salads always play a big part in my menus, no matter what the occasion. The recipes that I've developed for *Sensational Salads* are suitable for all types of tastes and menus.

This book is divided into chapters by ingredients—Greens; Vegetables; Fruit; Beans; Grains, Rice & Pasta; Seafood; and Poultry & Meat, plus a chapter on Vinaigrettes & Dressings. They include recipes that make the most of these ingredients and allow each and every one of them to shine, whether it's a simple fruit salad like Watermelon, Cucumber & Mint Salad for a summer afternoon snack, an elegant starter salad like Spinach & Arugula Salad with Pancetta & Warm Mushrooms or an elaborate main-course salad such as Grilled Pork & Mango Salad with Warm Asian Greens.

This book is designed for you to create fantastic salads for stylish meals and to entertain in a relaxed manner simply by using the best-quality ingredients available to you. Enjoy!

GREENS

Green salads have undergone quite a revolution. The days of making a salad with a wedge of iceberg lettuce and bottled dressing are long gone. Now that various and vibrantly colored fresh greens are available year-round, the possibilities for making delicious, healthful salads are limitless.

This chapter on greens includes superb recipes that will lend texture and beauty to any meal. They are enticing to the eye and will lighten and refresh the palate as well.

Classic Mixed Greens Salad

THIS IS MY ESSENTIAL GREEN SALAD RECIPE, BECAUSE IT WORKS WITH EVERY MEAL FOR EVERY OCCASION. YOU CAN KEEP IT SIMPLE WITH SALAD GREENS ALONE OR ADD ANY NUMBER OF FRESH, SEASONAL INGREDIENTS. LIKE A LITTLE BLACK DRESS, YOU CAN DRESS IT UP OR DOWN. THAT'S WHY I CALL IT A CLASSIC.

4 cups mixed salad greens

VINAIGRETTE:
1 tablespoon balsamic vinegar

3 tablespoons extra-virgin olive oil

Kosher salt and freshly ground black pepper

1. Put the salad greens in a large bowl.

2. In a small bowl, whisk together the vinegar and olive oil until well combined. Pour over the salad and toss well. Season to taste with salt and pepper and toss again.

3. Serve at once from the bowl or arrange on individual plates.

Serves 6

When shopping for greens, look for the very best-quality ones you can find. They must look and feel fresh and vibrant and show no signs of browning, yellowing, or rotting. Mixed greens, or mesclun, which I refer to throughout the book, are a mix of tender young greens.

Mixed Greens with Roasted Fennel, Pears & Parmesan Cheese

SLOW-ROASTED FENNEL AND PEARS TASTE AND LOOK WONDERFUL TOGETHER. ALTHOUGH ANY KIND OF PEAR WORKS WELL IN THIS RECIPE, IT IS ESPECIALLY GOOD WITH RIPE RED BARTLETTS. USE THE FINEST-QUALITY PARMESAN CHEESE YOU CAN FIND FOR GARNISHING THE SALAD.

2 tablespoons corn oil

**1 fennel bulb, trimmed
and thinly sliced**

**2 ripe pears, quartered, cored,
and thinly sliced**

2 large heads endive

4 cups mixed salad greens

VINAIGRETTE:

2 tablespoons red wine vinegar

1/3 cup extra-virgin olive oil

1 teaspoon herbes de Provence

**Kosher salt and freshly ground
black pepper**

1/2 cup shaved Parmesan cheese

1. Preheat the oven to 350°F.

2. Brush a baking sheet with 1 tablespoon of the corn oil. Add the fennel, toss to coat, and spread in an even layer. Brush a second baking sheet with the remaining 1 tablespoon corn oil. Add the pears, toss to coat, and spread in an even layer. Bake the fennel and the pears until tender, about 30 minutes.

3. Trim off the base of the endives, separate the leaves, and tear in half. Put in a large salad bowl, add the greens, and toss together.

4. In a small bowl, whisk together the vinegar and olive oil. Add the herbs and salt and pepper to taste and whisk well to combine. Pour half of the vinaigrette over the endive and greens and toss gently to coat.

5. Serve from the bowl or arrange on individual plates. Top with the roasted fennel and pears and drizzle with the remaining vinaigrette. Garnish with Parmesan shavings and additional ground pepper, if desired, and serve at once.

Serves 6

Mixed Greens with Goat Cheese & Walnuts

Here is a simple and delicious salad that works well with any meal. A drizzle of walnut oil adds the perfect finishing touch.

2 cups mixed salad greens

2 cups trimmed arugula,
  rinsed and dried

1 bunch watercress, stemmed

VINAIGRETTE:
1 tablespoon red wine vinegar

Pinch of sugar

3 tablespoons extra-virgin
  olive oil

Kosher salt and freshly ground
  black pepper

¾ cup crumbled goat cheese

½ cup walnuts, toasted
  (see page 17)

Walnut oil, for drizzling

1. Put the greens, arugula, and watercress in a large bowl.

2. In a small bowl, whisk together the vinegar and sugar. Add the olive oil and salt and pepper to taste and whisk until well combined. Pour over the greens and toss well.

3. Arrange the greens on a platter or individual plates. Top the salad with goat cheese and walnuts and drizzle with a bit of walnut oil. Serve at once.

Serves 6

Toasting Nuts

Toasted nuts have a richer taste and a crunchier texture than untoasted ones. Here are two easy methods for toasting nuts. Whichever one you use, watch the nuts carefully because they tend to burn quickly.

OVEN METHOD: To toast nuts in the oven, spread them on a baking sheet and toast them in a preheated 350°F oven or toaster oven for about 5 minutes until golden brown and fragrant. Shake the pan once or twice for even toasting. Slide the nuts off the baking sheet as soon as they reach the desired color to stop the cooking. Let them cool.

SKILLET METHOD: To toast nuts in a skillet, warm the skillet over medium heat, add the nuts, and stir or shake the pan frequently, until they just begin to brown and are fragrant, 2 to 3 minutes. Remove from the heat and slide them onto a plate. Let them cool. This method works well for a small quantity.

Boston & Romaine Lettuce
with Bacon, Tomatoes & Croutons

THIS TASTY SALAD, MADE WITH BACON, CHOPPED TOMATOES, AND CROUTONS, IS AS SATISFYING AS A CLUB SANDWICH OR A BLT FROM THE DINER. IN FACT, IT WOULD BE GREAT WITH A SIDE OF FRIES AND A COKE.

6 slices bacon

2 tablespoons olive oil

1 cup bread cubes (½ inch)

DRESSING:

¼ cup mayonnaise

1 tablespoon apple cider vinegar

1 tablespoon ketchup

1 tablespoon chopped sweet pickle

2 tablespoons chopped fresh flat-leaf parsley

Dash of hot sauce

Dash of Worcestershire sauce

Freshly ground black pepper

1 head Boston lettuce, tough outer leaves removed, inner leaves torn in half

½ head romaine lettuce, tough outer leaves removed, inner leaves torn in half

2 large ripe tomatoes, cut into ½-inch pieces

½ red onion, thinly sliced

1. Fry the bacon in a skillet or sauté pan until crisp and drain on paper towels. When cool enough to handle, crumble and set aside.

2. Wipe out the pan with paper towels. Heat the olive oil in the pan, add the bread cubes, and cook over medium-high heat, stirring often, until lightly browned, about 7 to 8 minutes. Turn the heat down if the bread is browning too fast. Drain on paper towels.

3. In a small bowl, mix the mayonnaise, vinegar, ketchup, pickle, parsley, hot sauce, Worcestershire sauce, and pepper until well combined. Taste and adjust the seasonings, if necessary.

4. Put the lettuce, tomatoes, onion, and half of the croutons in a large bowl and toss with half of the dressing. Pour the remaining dressing over the mixture and top with the crumbled bacon and the remaining croutons. Add a bit more fresh pepper, if desired. Serve at once from the bowl or arrange on individual plates.

Serves 6

Creamy Lemon Caesar Salad

ROMAINE-BASED CAESAR SALAD IS NOW REPUTED TO BE AMERICA'S MOST POPULAR SALAD, AND IT IS SERVED IN COUNTLESS WAYS. SOME DIE-HARD FANS OF THE CLASSIC CAESAR INSIST THAT ANCHOVIES ARE AN ESSENTIAL INGREDIENT IN THE SALAD DRESSING. THIS VERSION IS MADE WITH A CREAMY, LIGHT, AND LEMONY DRESSING, AND ANCHOVIES ARE OPTIONAL.

DRESSING:

2 cloves garlic, halved

1 tablespoon fresh lemon juice

1 teaspoon white wine vinegar

2/3 cup extra-virgin olive oil

3 tablespoons heavy cream

Kosher salt and freshly ground
black pepper

4 anchovies (optional)

2 tablespoons olive oil

1 cup bread cubes (1/2 inch)

1 head romaine lettuce, tough
outer leaves removed, inner
leaves torn in half

1/2 cup freshly grated Parmesan
cheese

Anchovies, for garnish (optional)

1. Put the garlic, lemon juice, and vinegar in a food processor. Process about 30 seconds. With the motor running, slowly add the extra-virgin olive oil through the feed tube and process until thick. Turn off the machine, add the cream, salt and pepper to taste, and anchovies, if using. Process again until well combined. The dressing will keep, covered, in the refrigerator, for up to 2 days before serving. Whisk well before serving.

2. Heat the olive oil in a skillet or sauté pan, add the bread cubes, and cook over medium-high heat, stirring often, until lightly browned, about 7 to 8 minutes. Turn the heat down if the bread is browning too fast. Drain on paper towels.

3. Put the lettuce in a large bowl. Add just enough dressing to moisten the lettuce (there will be some dressing left over) and toss to coat. Add the croutons, sprinkle with the cheese, and toss again. Taste and adjust the seasonings, if necessary. Serve at once from the bowl or arrange on individual plates. Garnish with additional anchovies, if desired.

Serves 6

Spinach & Arugula Salad
with Pancetta & Warm Mushrooms

THIS WARM AND WOODSY SALAD IS JUST THE THING TO EAT ON A CHILLY AUTUMN EVENING.

6 slices pancetta, about ⅛ inch thick, or 4 slices thick-cut bacon

7 tablespoons olive oil

½ pound shiitake mushrooms, stemmed and thinly sliced

½ pound domestic or cremini mushrooms, stemmed and thinly sliced

2 cloves garlic, thinly sliced

¼ cup **Niçoise olives**, pitted and halved

2 tablespoons drained capers

2 tablespoons fresh lemon juice

1 tablespoon balsamic vinegar

4 cups spinach or baby spinach, stemmed, rinsed, and patted dry

2 cups trimmed arugula, rinsed and dried

Freshly ground black pepper

¾ cup crumbled blue or Gorgonzola cheese

1. In a skillet or sauté pan, fry the pancetta or bacon over medium heat until crisp. Drain on paper towels, cut into small pieces, and set aside.

2. Wipe out the pan with paper towels. Heat 3 tablespoons of the olive oil in the pan over medium-high heat. Add the mushrooms and sauté, stirring frequently, for 5 minutes. Reduce the heat to medium and stir in the garlic, olives, capers, lemon juice, and vinegar. Simmer for 5 minutes to blend the flavors.

3. Meanwhile, toss the spinach and arugula with the remaining 4 tablespoons olive oil in a large bowl. Season to taste with pepper. Add the warm mushroom mixture and the pancetta or bacon to the greens and toss until well blended. Sprinkle with the cheese and serve at once from the bowl or arrange on individual plates.

Serves 6

Arugula & Apple Salad

THIS ELEGANT AND EASY SALAD IS NICE TO MAKE WITH THE SEASON'S FIRST SWEET-TART APPLES, SUCH AS MACOUN, MCINTOSH, OR NORTHERN SPY. YOU CAN ADD ALL KINDS OF GOOD THINGS TO IT, LIKE CHOPPED FENNEL, RED ONION, OR WALNUTS, IF YOU PREFER A MORE ELABORATE SALAD.

6 cups trimmed arugula, rinsed and dried

2 sweet-tart apples, cored and cut into 1-inch chunks

VINAIGRETTE:

1 tablespoon balsamic vinegar

3 tablespoons extra-virgin olive oil

1 tablespoon light cream

Kosher salt and freshly ground black pepper

1. Put the arugula and apples in a large salad bowl.

2. In a small bowl, whisk together the vinegar and olive oil. Slowly add the cream and salt and pepper to taste and whisk until well combined. Pour over the arugula and apples and toss well. Serve at once from the bowl or arrange on individual plates.

Serves 6

Arugula & Tomato Salad
with Ricotta Salata Cheese

THIS IS A LOVELY SALAD TO MAKE WITH SUMMER-FRESH ARUGULA AND CHERRY TOMATOES. I LIKE TO SERVE THIS GARNISHED WITH SLICES OF RICOTTA SALATA, A NUTTY-FLAVORED SHEEP'S-MILK CHEESE THAT IS A BIT LESS ASSERTIVE THAN FETA.

6 cups trimmed arugula, rinsed and dried

VINAIGRETTE:
1 tablespoon balsamic vinegar

3 tablespoons extra-virgin olive oil

1/2 cup cherry tomatoes

1/4 pound ricotta salata cheese, cut into 1/4-inch slices

2 tablespoons drained capers

1. Put the arugula in a large bowl.

2. In a small bowl, whisk together the vinegar and olive oil until well combined. Pour half of the vinaigrette over the arugula and toss to coat.

3. Arrange the greens on a platter or individual plates. Put the tomatoes and cheese over the greens and drizzle with the remaining vinaigrette. Sprinkle the salad with capers and serve at once.

Serves 6

VEGETABLES

All good cooks know that what's in season is the best guideline for planning their menus. This chapter includes a wide range of fresh vegetables and a variety of salads for all seasons— delicate springtime asparagus salad, summery cole slaws and garden-fresh tomato salads, and hearty cold-weather salads featuring roasted cauliflower, eggplant, and mushrooms.

Freshness is the heart and soul of the perfect salad, so take advantage of each season's bounty of vegetables. The wide selection of choices offers a fresh idea every day.

Warm Roasted Asparagus
& Shiitake Mushroom Salad

ROASTED ASPARAGUS AND WARM SHIITAKE MUSHROOMS ARE AN UNBEATABLE COMBINATION. THIS SALAD IS
DELICIOUS SERVED WITH A PIECE OF GRILLED CHICKEN OR STEAK.

**3 tablespoons extra-virgin
  olive oil**

2 pounds asparagus, trimmed

Kosher salt

2 cloves garlic, thinly sliced

**2 cups shiitake mushrooms,
  thinly sliced**

1 tablespoon fresh lemon juice

Freshly ground black pepper

4 cups mixed salad greens

1. Preheat the oven to 350°F.

2. Brush a baking sheet with 1 tablespoon of the olive oil,
put the asparagus on it, season to taste with the salt, and toss
to coat. Spread the asparagus in an even layer and roast until
tender and lightly browned, 30 to 40 minutes.

3. Heat the remaining 2 tablespoons olive oil in a large skillet
or sauté pan, add the garlic, and cook over medium heat until
softened, about 2 minutes. Add the mushrooms, lemon juice,
and salt and pepper to taste and cook until browned, 5 to 7
minutes. Remove from the heat.

4. Just before serving, reheat the mushrooms and add the
roasted asparagus. Cook over medium-high heat, tossing constantly, until heated through, 1 to 2 minutes. Taste and adjust
the seasonings, if necessary.

5. Arrange the salad greens on a platter and put the asparagus mixture over them. Add a bit more lemon juice, if desired,
and serve at once.

Serves 6

Green Bean, Yellow Bean & Red Pepper Salad

THIS SALAD IS A GREAT WAY TO APPRECIATE THE FULL FLAVORS OF FRESH BEANS AND RED PEPPERS IN SEASON. MAKE IT AHEAD OF TIME AND SERVE CHILLED OR MAKE SHORTLY BEFORE EATING AND SERVE AT ROOM TEMPERATURE.

¾ pound green beans, ends trimmed

¾ pound yellow beans, ends trimmed

2 red bell peppers, seeded, deveined, and cut into thin strips

VINAIGRETTE:

2 tablespoons Dijon mustard

2 tablespoons balsamic vinegar

2 tablespoons light soy sauce

½ cup extra-virgin olive oil

Kosher salt and freshly ground black pepper

¼ cup chopped fresh flat-leaf parsley, for garnish

1. Cook the green and yellow beans in enough lightly salted boiling water to cover for about 2 minutes, until crisp-tender. Drain and rinse under cold running water. Drain again.

2. In another pot, cook the peppers in enough lightly salted boiling water to cover for about 3 minutes, until just tender. Drain and rinse under cold running water. Drain again.

3. Combine the beans and peppers in a large bowl.

4. In a small bowl, mix together the mustard, vinegar, and soy sauce. Slowly whisk in the olive oil until the vinaigrette thickens. Season to taste with salt and pepper.

5. Pour the dressing over the vegetables and toss well. Chill the salad or serve it at room temperature. Garnish with fresh parsley just before serving.

Serves 6

Celery Root, Roasted Beet & Apple Salad

CELERY ROOT—ALSO KNOWN AS CELERIAC OR CELERY KNOB—IS A DELICIOUS ROOT VEGETABLE, AND IT IS ESPECIALLY GOOD WHEN PAIRED WITH ROASTED BEETS. TO PREPARE IT, TRIM THE ENDS, PEEL THE BULB, AND SHRED IT FINELY IN A FOOD PROCESSOR. THIS HEARTY SALAD IS WONDERFUL TO SERVE FOR AN AUTUMN OR WINTER DINNER AS A STARTER OR AS A SIDE DISH WITH ROAST LOIN OF PORK OR VEAL CHOPS.

6 beets (about 2 pounds), trimmed, leaving 1-inch stem attached

1 celery root, peeled and finely shredded (about 3 cups)

VINAIGRETTE:

2 tablespoons fresh lemon juice

2 tablespoons minced shallot

$1/4$ cup extra-virgin olive oil

Kosher salt and freshly ground black pepper

1 Granny Smith apple, cored and cut into 1-inch pieces

$1/2$ cup walnuts, toasted (see page 17)

1. Preheat the oven to 425°F.

2. Wrap the beets tightly in foil to make 2 packages (3 beets in each) and roast until tender, about 1$1/4$ hours. While the beets roast, put the celery root in a large bowl.

3. In a small bowl, whisk together the lemon juice, shallot, olive oil, and salt and pepper to taste until well combined. Pour over the celery root and toss until well coated. Cover and keep at room temperature until the beets are ready.

4. Carefully unwrap the beets and, when just cool enough to handle, slip off the skins and remove the stems. Cut the beets into $1/8$-inch-thick julienne and toss with the celery root.

5. Let the salad stand, covered, at room temperature for 1 hour. Taste and adjust the seasonings, adding more lemon juice, salt, and pepper, if necessary.

6. Just before serving, add the apple and walnuts and toss again. Serve at once.

Serves 6

Carrot, Pepper & Scallion Salad

SHREDDED CARROTS, BELL PEPPER, AND SCALLIONS COMBINE BEAUTIFULLY IN THIS REFRESHING SUMMERY SALAD. IT CAN BE MADE WELL AHEAD OF TIME AND SERVED WITH GRILLED PORK OR CHICKEN.

**3 cups shredded carrots
(about 6 carrots)**

**1 red or yellow bell pepper,
seeded, deveined, and diced**

4 scallions, trimmed and minced

**2 tablespoons chopped
fresh mint**

VINAIGRETTE:

3 tablespoons fresh lemon juice

1/2 teaspoon ground cumin

1/2 teaspoon paprika

1 teaspoon brown sugar

1 clove garlic, finely minced

**3 tablespoons extra-virgin
olive oil**

**Kosher salt and freshly ground
black pepper**

1. Put the carrots, bell pepper, scallions, and mint in a large bowl and toss to combine.

2. In a small bowl, mix together the lemon juice, cumin, paprika, sugar, and garlic. Add the olive oil, whisking constantly, until well combined. Pour over the carrot mixture, season to taste with salt and pepper, and toss well. Cover and chill the salad for a few hours or overnight.

3. Taste and adjust the seasonings, if necessary. Add a bit more lemon juice and mint, if desired. Toss again and serve.

Serves 6

Roasted Cauliflower Salad

CAULIFLOWER MAY BE AN ACQUIRED TASTE FOR SOME PEOPLE, BUT WHEN IT IS ROASTED WITH RED PEPPERS AND TOSSED WITH A ZESTY BLEND OF WARM OLIVE OIL, OLIVES, AND CAPERS, IT TAKES ON A DELICIOUS NUTTY FLAVOR THAT IS HARD FOR ANYONE TO PASS UP. SERVE THIS AS A SIDE SALAD WITH ALMOST ANY DISH OR AS PART OF AN ANTIPASTO PLATTER.

2 heads cauliflower, cut into florets

Kosher salt and freshly ground black pepper

About 1 cup olive oil

1 red bell pepper, seeded, deveined, and cut into thin strips

1 tablespoon grated lemon zest

2 cloves garlic, thinly sliced

1/4 cup kalamata olives, pitted and chopped

2 tablespoons drained capers

Lemon wedges, for garnish

1. Preheat the oven to 350°F.

2. Put the cauliflower in a large bowl and season to taste with salt and pepper. Pour 1/3 cup of the olive oil over it and toss well. Spread the cauliflower on a baking sheet and roast, turning occasionally, until tender and golden brown, about 45 minutes. Transfer to a large bowl.

3. Put the pepper strips on a baking sheet; pour 2 tablespoons of the olive oil over them and toss well. Spread evenly and roast, turning occasionally, until tender, 40 to 45 minutes. Set aside until cool enough to handle. Dice the peppers and add to the cauliflower.

4. Meanwhile, combine the lemon zest, garlic, and 1/2 cup of the olive oil in a small saucepan and cook over low heat, stirring occasionally, about 20 minutes.

5. Pour the warm olive oil over the cauliflower mixture and toss. Add the olives and capers and toss again. Season to taste with additional black pepper. Serve on a platter, garnished with lemon wedges.

Serves 6 to 8

Cucumber-Mint Raita

RAITA, A YOGURT-BASED INDIAN DISH, CAN BE CONSIDERED A SALAD, A SIDE DISH, OR A CONDIMENT. ITS LIGHT AND CREAMY COOLNESS COMPLEMENTS SPICY DISHES, AND IT IS VERY REFRESHING. I LIKE TO MAKE THIS WITH LOW-FAT PLAIN YOGURT, WHICH SHOULD BE DRAINED BEFORE USING TO MAKE IT LESS WATERY. IT IS EXCELLENT WITH GRILLED LAMB, CHICKEN, OR SEAFOOD.

2 cups low-fat plain yogurt

1 teaspoon ground cumin

Pinch of crushed red pepper flakes

Pinch of sugar

Kosher salt and freshly ground black pepper

3 large cucumbers or 8 small kirby cucumbers, peeled, seeded, and diced

1/2 red onion, finely diced

1/2 cup chopped fresh mint

1. Put the yogurt in a strainer lined with cheesecloth or a paper towel over a bowl. Drain for 15 minutes and transfer to a medium bowl. Add the cumin, red pepper flakes, sugar, and salt and pepper to taste and whisk together until creamy and well combined.

2. Put the cucumbers, onion, and mint in a large bowl and toss together. Pour the yogurt mixture over them and toss well to combine. Taste and adjust the seasonings. Cover and chill the raita for a few hours before serving.

Serves 6

Ruby Red Slaw

This sweet and spicy slaw, subtly flavored with orange and lime juice, is a great-looking, delicious accompaniment to grilled chicken, ribs, or fish.

1 small head red cabbage,
  cored and thinly sliced

1 red bell pepper, seeded,
  deveined, and thinly sliced

1 red onion, thinly sliced

VINAIGRETTE:

2 tablespoons red wine vinegar

3 tablespoons orange juice

1 tablespoon fresh lime juice

1/3 cup mayonnaise

1 teaspoon ground cumin

1/2 cup extra-virgin olive oil

Kosher salt and freshly ground
  black pepper

1/4 cup chopped fresh flat-leaf
  parsley, for garnish

1. Put the cabbage, bell pepper, and onion in a large bowl. Toss together until well combined.

2. In a medium bowl, mix together the vinegar, orange juice, and lime juice. Gently stir in the mayonnaise and cumin until well combined. Whisk in the olive oil until the vinaigrette is creamy and thickened and all of the oil has been incorporated.

3. Pour the vinaigrette over the cabbage mixture and toss well. Add salt and pepper to taste and mix well again. Cover and chill the slaw until ready to serve.

4. Taste and adjust the seasonings, if necessary. Garnish with parsley and serve.

Serves 8 to 10

Creamy Cabbage Slaw

THERE'S NOTHING BETTER TO BRING TO A SUMMER BARBECUE OR PICNIC THAN CLASSIC COLE SLAW WITH CREAMY MAYONNAISE DRESSING. THIS RECIPE USES A COMBINATION OF GREEN CABBAGE AND CHINESE OR NAPA CABBAGE. CHINESE CABBAGE HAS A LIGHT, DELICATE FLAVOR THAT BLENDS WELL WITH ALL OF THE OTHER INGREDIENTS IN THIS DISH. I LIKE TO MAKE THIS SLAW A FEW HOURS AHEAD OF TIME AND LET THE FLAVORS INTENSIFY AS IT CHILLS.

½ head green cabbage, finely shredded

½ head Chinese or napa cabbage, finely shredded

2 carrots, finely shredded

Kosher salt and freshly ground black pepper

DRESSING:

¾ cup mayonnaise

1 teaspoon Dijon mustard

1½ teaspoons sugar

1 tablespoon white vinegar

½ teaspoon celery seed

½ teaspoon paprika

1. Put the cabbages and carrots in a large bowl, add salt and pepper to taste, and toss well to combine.

2. In a medium bowl, stir together the mayonnaise, mustard, sugar, vinegar, celery seed, and paprika until well combined. Pour the dressing over the cabbage mixture and toss gently to combine. Season to taste with salt and pepper. Cover and chill the slaw until ready to serve.

3. Taste and adjust the seasonings, if necessary, and serve.

Serves 6 to 8

Fennel & Red Onion Slaw

THIS WONDERFUL AND REFRESHING VERSION OF COLE SLAW IS MADE WITH CRUNCHY FENNEL
AND RED ONIONS. WHEN BUYING FENNEL, LOOK FOR BULBS WITH THEIR STALKS INTACT. PRESS
THE FLESH OF THE BULB TO TEST FOR FRESHNESS; IT SHOULD FEEL FIRM AND RESIST GENTLE PRESSURE.

**2 large fennel bulbs, trimmed
and very thinly sliced**

1 red onion, thinly sliced

VINAIGRETTE:

3 tablespoons balsamic vinegar

2 tablespoons light soy sauce

2 tablespoons fresh lemon juice

1 tablespoon orange juice

**1 tablespoon finely minced
ginger**

$1/3$ cup extra-virgin olive oil

**Kosher salt and freshly ground
black pepper**

**$1/2$ cup chopped fresh flat-leaf
parsley**

1. Put the fennel and onion in a large bowl.

2. In a small bowl, mix together the vinegar, soy sauce,
lemon juice, orange juice, and ginger. Slowly add the olive oil,
whisking constantly, until the vinaigrette thickens. Pour over
the fennel mixture and toss. Season to taste with salt and
pepper. Cover and chill the slaw until ready to serve.

3. Add the parsley and toss again. Taste and adjust the
seasonings, if necessary, and serve.

Serves 6 to 8

Caponata Salad

LIKE RAITA, CAPONATA ALSO CAN BE CLASSIFIED AS A SALAD, SIDE DISH, OR CONDIMENT. MADE WITH ROASTED EGGPLANT AND ONION AND MIXED WITH FRESH TOMATOES, HERBS, CAPERS, AND CHOPPED OLIVES, IT IS DELICIOUS, NO MATTER WHAT YOU CALL IT. THIS VERSATILE DISH IS VERY GOOD SERVED ON GREENS AS A STARTER SALAD, AS AN ACCOMPANIMENT TO LAMB OR PORK, OR AS PART OF A BUFFET.

2 eggplants, peeled and cut into ½-inch-thick slices

1 red onion, cut into ½-inch-thick slices

¼ cup olive oil

1 ripe tomato or 4 plum tomatoes, cut into cubes

3 tablespoons drained capers

½ cup pitted and chopped kalamata olives

½ cup pitted and chopped green olives

1 jalapeño pepper, seeded and minced

½ cup chopped fresh basil leaves

½ cup chopped fresh flat-leaf parsley

1½ tablespoons balsamic vinegar

2 tablespoons extra-virgin olive oil

Kosher salt and freshly ground black pepper

1. Preheat the oven to 400°F.

2. Brush the eggplant and onion slices with the olive oil and arrange on separate baking sheets in single layers. Roast, turning once, until soft and lightly browned, about 30 to 40 minutes. Remove from the oven and let cool.

3. Put the tomato, capers, kalamata and green olives, and jalapeño in a large bowl.

4. Chop the roasted eggplant and onion into coarse chunks and add to the tomato mixture. Add the basil, parsley, vinegar, and extra-virgin olive oil and toss gently. Season to taste with salt and pepper and toss again. Cover and chill for 6 to 8 hours or overnight.

5. Before serving, taste and adjust the seasonings, if necessary. Serve chilled or at room temperature.

Serves 6

Grilled Portobello Mushroom & Goat Cheese Salad

RICH AND LUSH GRILLED PORTOBELLO MUSHROOMS TASTE FANTASTIC WHEN THEY ARE COMBINED WITH RED ONIONS, OLIVE OIL, AND BALSAMIC VINEGAR AND TOPPED WITH GOAT CHEESE.

6 large portobello mushrooms, stemmed

¾ cup plus 2 tablespoons extra-virgin olive oil

2 cloves garlic, thinly sliced

Kosher salt and freshly ground black pepper

½ red onion, thinly sliced lengthwise

1 tablespoon balsamic vinegar

2 tablespoons chopped fresh flat-leaf parsley

4 cups mixed salad greens

½ cup crumbled herbed goat cheese

1. Arrange the mushrooms in 1 layer in a large shallow bowl. Pour ¾ cup of the olive oil over them. Sprinkle with the garlic and salt and pepper to taste. Cover loosely and let marinate for about 2 hours.

2. Prepare a charcoal or gas grill. Spray the grill rack with cooking spray. When the fire is medium-hot (coals are covered with a light coating of ash and glow deep red), remove the mushrooms from the marinade and grill until golden and lightly charred, about 4 minutes per side.

3. Cut the mushrooms into thick slices and transfer to a large bowl. Add the onion, vinegar, parsley, the remaining 2 tablespoons olive oil, and salt and pepper to taste and toss well to combine. Taste and adjust the seasonings, if necessary.

4. Arrange the salad greens on a platter or divide among individual plates. Spoon the mushroom salad over them and sprinkle with the goat cheese. Drizzle with additional olive oil and pepper, if desired, and serve at once.

Serves 6

POTATOES FOR SALAD

With so many varieties of potatoes available, which are best for making potato salad? As a rule, low-starch potatoes, such as new red potatoes, long whites, and fingerlings, are more suitable for using in salads, because they retain their firmness after cooking. High-starch potatoes, such as russets, are more absorbent and may fall apart when boiled.

It is preferable not to peel potatoes before cooking them for salad, because unpeeled potatoes retain their shape better and will not become soggy. Another benefit of cooking potatoes in their skins is that more nutrients are retained.

POTATO BASICS

• Select potatoes that are about the same size, so that they will cook uniformly. If potatoes are very large, they may take longer to cook, so cut them into same-size pieces before cooking.

• When buying potatoes, buy what you're planning to use within a week to 10 days.

• Don't buy potatoes with sprouted "eyes," which are a product of age. Also pass up potatoes with green spots or blemishes.

• Store potatoes in a cool, dry place.

• Do not refrigerate potatoes, because refrigeration turns their starches to sugars.

• Never freeze potatoes.

Country Potato Salad with Chopped Egg, Ham & Pickles

THIS HEARTY POTATO SALAD IS BASED ON AN OLD SOUTHERN COUNTRY RECIPE. IT'S FANTASTIC WITH BARBECUED RIBS OR CHICKEN AND CORN ON THE COB.

2½ to 3 pounds small red potatoes

½ cup chopped red onion

2 hard-cooked eggs, chopped

½ cup diced celery

½ cup diced ham

½ cup diced sweet pickle

DRESSING:

1 cup mayonnaise

½ cup sour cream

1 tablespoon Dijon mustard

Kosher salt and freshly ground black pepper

½ cup chopped fresh dill

½ cup chopped fresh flat-leaf parsley

1. Put the potatoes in a large pot of boiling salted water and cook until they are fork-tender, 20 to 25 minutes. Rinse, drain, and let cool.

2. Peel the potatoes, if desired, and cut into ½-inch pieces. Put the potatoes, onion, eggs, celery, ham, and pickle in a large bowl.

3. In a medium bowl, mix together the mayonnaise, sour cream, mustard, and salt and pepper to taste. Fold the dressing into the potato mixture and toss gently but thoroughly. Add the dill and parsley and toss again. Taste and adjust the seasonings, if necessary. Serve chilled or at room temperature.

Serves 6 to 8

Roasted Potato Salad
with Arugula & Goat Cheese

THIS SALAD ALWAYS WINS RAVES FROM MY GUESTS. BE SURE TO ROAST THE POTATOES SLOWLY IN A 300°F OVEN. SLOW COOKING GIVES THE GARLIC AND OIL TIME TO INFUSE THE POTATOES WITH THEIR ENTICING FLAVORS. ALSO, BE SURE TO MIX THE VINAIGRETTE WITH THE POTATOES WHILE THEY ARE STILL WARM.

2 1/2 pounds small red potatoes, halved or quartered, depending on size

8 unpeeled cloves garlic

Kosher salt

1/3 cup olive oil

VINAIGRETTE:

2 teaspoons whole-grain mustard

1 tablespoon balsamic vinegar

1/2 cup extra-virgin olive oil

3/4 to 1 cup trimmed arugula, rinsed and dried

1/2 cup crumbled goat cheese

Freshly ground black pepper

2 teaspoons extra-virgin olive oil

1. Preheat the oven to 300°F.

2. In a roasting pan, toss together the potatoes, garlic, salt to taste, and olive oil. Bake for 1 1/2 to 2 hours, until the potatoes are fork-tender. Check the potatoes every so often; if they stick to the bottom of the pan, scrape them from the pan and gently toss them with the other ingredients. Lower the heat to 250°F if the potatoes are cooking too quickly.

3. In a small bowl, whisk together the mustard and vinegar. Slowly add 1/2 cup extra-virgin olive oil, whisking constantly, until the vinaigrette thickens.

4. Remove the potatoes from the oven and scrape them into a large bowl. Pour the vinaigrette over the warm potatoes and gently toss them with the dressing. Add the arugula and toss again.

5. Heap the potato salad into a large shallow bowl or on a platter. Sprinkle the crumbled cheese over the top. Season to taste with pepper and drizzle with 2 teaspoons extra-virgin olive oil. Serve the salad warm or at room temperature.

Serves 6

Red Potato, Green Bean & Dill Salad

THERE ARE SO MANY DELICIOUS WAYS TO PREPARE POTATO SALAD AND THIS VERSION, MADE WITH FRESH
GREEN BEANS AND DILL AND A TANGY VINAIGRETTE, IS A WINNER.

2$\frac{1}{2}$ to 3 pounds small red
  potatoes, halved or quartered,
  depending on size

I pound green beans, trimmed
  and cut into 2-inch pieces

$\frac{1}{2}$ red onion, thinly sliced

VINAIGRETTE:

2 tablespoons Dijon mustard

2 tablespoons whole-grain
  mustard

I tablespoon white vinegar

I tablespoon fresh lemon juice

$\frac{1}{3}$ cup extra-virgin olive oil

$\frac{1}{2}$ cup chopped fresh dill

Kosher salt and freshly ground
  black pepper

1. Put the potatoes in a large pot of boiling salted water and cook until they are fork-tender, about 20 minutes. Drain and cool and put them in a large bowl.

2. Put the beans in a medium pot of boiling salted water and simmer until just crisp-tender, about 2 minutes. Drain and cool. Add the beans and onion to the potatoes.

3. In a small bowl, whisk together the mustards, vinegar, and lemon juice. Slowly add the olive oil, whisking constantly, until the vinaigrette thickens.

4. Pour the vinaigrette over the potato mixture and toss. Add the dill and salt and pepper to taste and toss again. Taste and adjust the seasonings, if necessary, and serve at room temperature.

Serves 6 to 8

Fingerling Potato, Smoked Salmon & Dill Salad

FINGERLING POTATOES ARE SMALL, LONG POTATOES WITH BROWN, RED, OR PURPLE SKINS. THEY ARE RATHER DELICATE AND COOK QUITE QUICKLY, SO WATCH THEM CLOSELY WHILE THEY'RE BOILING TO MAKE SURE THEY DON'T BECOME MUSHY. FINGERLINGS MAKE THIS SALAD RICH, INDULGENT, AND FANTASTIC.

2½ pounds fingerling potatoes

½ cup chopped fresh dill

VINAIGRETTE:

1 tablespoon Dijon mustard

1 tablespoon whole-grain mustard

1 tablespoon white vinegar

1 teaspoon sugar

⅓ cup extra-virgin olive oil

⅓ pound smoked salmon, cut into small pieces

Freshly ground black pepper

1. Put the potatoes in a large pot of boiling salted water and cook until they are fork-tender, 15 to 20 minutes. Drain and cool. Cut the potatoes in half lengthwise and put them in a large bowl. Add half of the dill and toss well.

2. In a small bowl, whisk together the mustards, vinegar, and sugar. Slowly add the olive oil, whisking constantly, until the vinaigrette thickens. Pour about half of the vinaigrette over the potatoes and toss gently to coat. Add the smoked salmon and the remaining vinaigrette and season to taste with the pepper. Taste and adjust the seasonings, if necessary. Garnish with the remaining dill and serve at room temperature.

Serves 6

Snap Pea & Orange Salad

ORANGE JUICE, RICE VINEGAR, AND FRESH GINGER ARE THE KEY VINAIGRETTE INGREDIENTS IN THIS LIGHT AND LOVELY SUMMER SALAD MADE WITH CRUNCHY SNAP PEAS. SNOW PEAS MAY BE SUBSTITUTED FOR THE SNAP PEAS.

1 pound sugar snap peas, trimmed

1 orange, peeled and cut into 1-inch pieces

3 scallions, trimmed and minced

VINAIGRETTE:

1 teaspoon Dijon mustard

1 teaspoon rice vinegar

2 teaspoons grated orange zest

1 tablespoon fresh orange juice

1 tablespoon finely grated ginger

⅓ cup extra-virgin olive oil

1. Cook the snap peas in enough lightly salted water to cover until crisp-tender, about 2 minutes. Drain and rinse under cold water. Drain again. Transfer to a large bowl and add the orange and scallions.

2. In a small bowl, whisk together the mustard, vinegar, orange zest, orange juice, and ginger. Slowly add the olive oil, whisking constantly, until the vinaigrette thickens.

3. Pour the vinaigrette over the snap pea mixture and toss to combine. Chill the salad for a few hours before serving.

Serves 6

Summer Tomatoes with Gorgonzola Cheese

THERE IS NOTHING SIMPLER TO PREPARE OR MORE DELICIOUS TO EAT THAN A PLATTER OF SUMMER-RIPE RED TOMATOES TOPPED WITH PUNGENT GORGONZOLA CHEESE AND A DRIZZLE OF EXTRA-VIRGIN OLIVE OIL. SERVE WITH OLIVES AND CRUSTY PEASANT BREAD. THAT'S IT!

6 large ripe tomatoes (about 3 pounds), thickly sliced

VINAIGRETTE:

2 tablespoons red wine vinegar

6 tablespoons extra-virgin olive oil

Kosher salt and freshly ground black pepper

¾ cup crumbled Gorgonzola cheese

1. Arrange the tomato slices in an overlapping pattern on a serving dish.

2. In a medium bowl, whisk together the vinegar, olive oil, and salt and pepper to taste and blend well. Add the cheese and gently mash it with a fork. The vinaigrette should be slightly lumpy.

3. Pour the vinaigrette over the tomatoes. Season to taste with additional pepper and serve immediately.

Serves 6 to 8

Grilled Bread, Cherry Tomato & Basil Salad

I AM AN AVOWED TOMATO FANATIC, AND I LOVE TO MAKE THIS SALAD WITH FRESH RED AND YELLOW CHERRY TOMATOES WHEN THEY ARE AT THEIR PEAK OF RIPENESS. THIS SIMPLE AND STRAIGHTFORWARD RECIPE ALLOWS EVERY INGREDIENT TO SHINE.

One 12-inch baguette, halved lengthwise

5 tablespoons extra-virgin olive oil

1 1/4 pounds red and yellow cherry tomatoes, halved (about 3 cups)

1/4 cup kalamata olives, pitted and halved

1/4 cup fresh basil leaves, thinly sliced

1 small bunch watercress, stemmed

1 small bunch arugula, trimmed, rinsed, and dried

Freshly ground black pepper

1. Preheat the broiler. Brush the baguette halves with 2 tablespoons of the olive oil and put on a baking sheet. Grill the bread until golden brown, 3 to 5 minutes. Remove and let cool. Cut the bread into 1-inch cubes.

2. Put the bread, tomatoes, olives, basil, watercress, and arugula in a large bowl and toss. Add the remaining 3 tablespoons olive oil and toss again.

3. Allow the mixture to sit for about 1/2 hour so the bread can soak up the juices. If the mixture seems too dry, add a bit more olive oil to taste and toss again. Season to taste with pepper and serve.

Serves 6

Heirloom Tomato & Mozzarella Cheese Salad

HEIRLOOM TOMATOES ARE SO CALLED BECAUSE THEIR SEEDS HAVE BEEN PASSED DOWN THROUGH GENERATIONS OF GROWERS' FAMILIES. THEY ARE DEFINITELY WORTH SEEKING OUT AT YOUR LOCAL FARMERS' MARKET. THEIR UNIQUE SHAPES AND VIBRANT COLORS—YELLOW, ORANGE, WHITE, AND SHADES OF GREEN AND PURPLE—ARE BEAUTIFUL IN SALADS, LIKE THIS VERY SIMPLE ONE MADE WITH MOZZARELLA CHEESE. USE THE FINEST-QUALITY INGREDIENTS YOU CAN FIND TO INTENSIFY THEIR FLAVOR.

6 assorted ripe heirloom tomatoes (about 3 pounds), cut into large wedges

$1/2$ red onion, thinly sliced

1 cup cubed fresh mozzarella cheese

1 tablespoon balsamic vinegar

3 tablespoons extra-virgin olive oil

Kosher salt and freshly ground black pepper

1. Put the tomatoes, onion, and cheese in a large bowl and toss gently to combine.

2. In a small bowl, whisk together the vinegar and oil until well blended. Pour over the tomato mixture and gently toss to combine. Season to taste with salt and pepper. Do not chill or let the salad sit for more than $1/2$ hour. Serve at room temperature.

Serves 6

Gazpacho Salad

Gazpacho is always the right thing to serve on sweltering summer days. In this recipe, I've taken all the elements of the chilled soup—vine-ripened tomatoes and farm-fresh cucumbers and peppers—and tossed them into a salad topped with golden, garlicky croutons. It's a simple-to-prepare, tasty twist on a classic.

2 large ripe tomatoes, coarsely chopped

3 small cucumbers, peeled, seeded, and coarsely chopped

1 green bell pepper, seeded, deveined, and diced

1 red bell pepper, seeded, deveined, and diced

3 scallions, trimmed and minced

1/2 cup chopped fresh flat-leaf parsley

1 teaspoon red wine vinegar

1 teaspoon balsamic vinegar

3 tablespoons olive oil

2 cloves garlic, thinly sliced

3 cups bread cubes (1/2 inch)

Kosher salt and freshly ground black pepper

Romaine lettuce leaves, for serving

1. Put the tomatoes, cucumbers, green and red peppers, scallions, parsley, and vinegars in a large bowl and toss gently to combine. Cover and chill for 3 or 4 hours.

2. Heat 2 tablespoons of the olive oil in a skillet or sauté pan, add the garlic, and cook over medium heat until golden, about 2 minutes. Add the bread cubes and cook over medium-high heat, stirring often, until lightly browned, about 7 to 8 minutes. Turn the heat down if the bread is browning too fast. Drain on paper towels.

3. Remove the salad from the refrigerator, add the remaining 1 tablespoon olive oil and salt and pepper to taste; stir gently but well. Taste and adjust the seasonings, if necessary.

4. To serve, divide the lettuce leaves among shallow soup bowls. Spoon the salad over them and top with the croutons.

Serves 6

FRUIT

Fruit salads can be incredibly tasty and interesting when you go beyond the standard cut-up apples, oranges, and grapes. It's fun to explore and experiment with different ingredients.

Try surprising combinations like grapefruit and avocados or market-fresh watermelon and cucumbers. These salads are always a delight to serve on hot summer days. When the weather turns cool, seek out fresh figs and crisp apples and pears for tossing with greens, cheese, and toasted nuts for delicious autumn and winter salads. It's all about using the best ingredients available to you.

Grapefruit, Orange & Avocado Salad

GRAPEFRUIT, ORANGES, AND AVOCADOS ARE A SURPRISING AND DELICIOUS COMBINATION. THIS IS A GOOD, TANGY SALAD TO SERVE IN THE WINTER WHEN ALL OF THESE FRUITS ARE AT THEIR BEST.

2 small grapefruits, peeled and cut into sections

2 oranges, peeled and cut into sections

2 avocados, pitted, peeled, and cut into bite-sized pieces

VINAIGRETTE:

1 teaspoon Dijon mustard

1 tablespoon white wine vinegar

2 tablespoons fresh grapefruit juice

4 tablespoons extra-virgin olive oil

Kosher salt

2 heads endive

1. Put the grapefruit sections, orange sections, and avocado pieces in a large bowl.

2. In a small bowl, whisk together the mustard, vinegar, and grapefruit juice. Slowly add the olive oil, whisking constantly, until the vinaigrette is thickened. Pour the vinaigrette over the fruit mixture and toss gently. Season with salt to taste. Taste and adjust the seasonings, if necessary, and toss again.

3. Arrange the endive leaves on a large platter or on individual plates. Spoon the fruit mixture over them and serve at once.

Serves 6

Watermelon, Cucumber & Mint Salad

WHEN WATERMELON IS IN SEASON THERE IS NOTHING COOLER LOOKING OR MORE REFRESHING THAN THIS SUMMER SALAD.

4 cups (about 3 pounds) seedless watermelon, cut into 1-inch cubes

2 cups seedless kirby cucumbers, peeled and cut into ½-inch cubes

VINAIGRETTE:

2 tablespoons fresh lime juice

2 tablespoons extra-virgin olive oil

Kosher salt

¼ cup chopped fresh mint

1 small bunch watercress, stemmed

¼ cup pine nuts

1. Put the watermelon and cucumbers in a large bowl.

2. Whisk together the lime juice, olive oil, and a pinch of salt. Pour over the watermelon mixture and toss to coat.

3. Add the mint, watercress, and pine nuts and toss again. Chill the salad for 1 hour before serving.

Serves 6

Tropical Fruit Salad

SERVE THIS DELIGHTFUL FRESH-FRUIT SALAD FOR BREAKFAST OR PACK IT INTO A COOLER FOR A TASTY SNACK AT THE BEACH.

1 **pineapple, trimmed, peeled, and cut into bite-sized pieces**

1 **papaya, trimmed, peeled, and cut into bite-sized pieces**

3 **kiwis, trimmed, peeled, and cut into bite-sized pieces**

1 **tablespoon brown sugar**

3 **tablespoons pineapple juice**

1. Put the pineapple, papaya, and kiwis in a large bowl and toss together.

2. In a small bowl, whisk together the sugar and pineapple juice until well blended. Pour over the fruit salad and toss. Chill the salad a few hours before serving.

Serves 6

Mango, Blueberry & Ginger Salad

MANGOES AND BLUEBERRIES ARE A LUSCIOUS COMBINATION, WITH ONE FRUIT COMPLEMENTING THE OTHER PERFECTLY IN BOTH TASTE AND LOOKS. MINCED GINGER AND FRESH LIME JUICE ADD PIQUANT FLAVOR TO THIS SUMMERY SALAD. ALTHOUGH YOU CAN USE REGULAR LIMES IN THIS RECIPE, IT TASTES FANTASTIC WITH KEY LIMES.

2 mangoes, peeled, pitted, and cut into 1-inch pieces

1 cup fresh blueberries

1 tablespoon minced ginger

2 tablespoons fresh lime juice, preferably from Key limes

Put the mangoes and blueberries in a large bowl. Add the ginger and lime juice and mix together. Cover and chill for at least 1 hour before serving.

Serves 6

Orange, Jicama & Watercress Salad

THE RAW JICAMA GIVES THIS LIGHT AND REFRESHING SALAD A WONDERFULLY CRUNCHY TEXTURE.
IT IS AN IDEAL DISH FOR WARM-WEATHER PICNICS AND BARBECUES.

3 oranges, peeled and cut into
  1-inch pieces

3 jicama (about 2 pounds),
  peeled and cut into thin strips,
  about 2½ inches long

1 red onion, thinly sliced

1 bunch watercress, stemmed

⅓ cup pine nuts, toasted
  (see page 17)

2 tablespoons fresh lime juice

VINAIGRETTE:

⅓ cup red wine vinegar

1 teaspoon ground cumin

Kosher salt and freshly ground
  black pepper

½ cup extra-virgin olive oil

1 head Boston lettuce, tough
  outer leaves removed,
  for serving

1. Put the oranges, jicama, onion, watercress, and pine nuts in a large bowl. Add the lime juice and toss well.

2. In a small bowl, whisk together the vinegar, cumin, and salt and pepper to taste. Slowly add the olive oil, whisking constantly, until the vinaigrette is thickened. Pour the vinaigrette over the orange mixture and toss. Taste and adjust the seasonings, if necessary, and toss again.

3. Arrange the lettuce leaves in a large shallow bowl or on a platter. Spoon the salad over the lettuce and serve at once.

Serves 6

Minted Summer Fruit Dessert Salad

THERE IS NOTHING BETTER THAN A SUMMER FRUIT SALAD MADE WITH FRESH PEACHES, PLUMS, AND MELON AT THE PEAK OF THEIR FRESHNESS. THIS IS SO GOOD I SERVE IT FOR DESSERT WITH A DOLLOP OF YOGURT MIXED WITH SOUR CREAM AND A DRIZZLE OF HONEY.

3 ripe peaches, peeled, pitted, and sliced

6 small ripe plums, pitted and sliced

1/2 ripe melon, such as honeydew, cantaloupe, or Crenshaw, seeded and cut into 1/2-inch cubes or balls (about 2 cups)

1/4 cup chopped fresh mint

1 cup low-fat plain yogurt

3 tablespoons low-fat sour cream

Honey, for drizzling

Mint leaves, for garnish

1. Put the peaches, plums, melon, and mint in a large bowl and toss together (see Note). Chill for a few hours.

2. Put the yogurt in a strainer lined with cheesecloth or a paper towel over a bowl. Drain for 15 minutes and transfer to a small bowl. Add the sour cream and mix well. Chill until ready to serve.

3. Spoon the fruit salad into dessert bowls or plates. Top each serving with a spoonful of the yogurt mixture and drizzle with honey. Garnish each serving with mint leaves and serve.

Serves 6

Note: The flavor of mint intensifies over time. If you prefer a less minty flavor, add the mint to the salad about an hour before serving.

Roasted Fig & Greens Salad with Stilton Cheese

THIS DELICIOUS RECIPE WAS INSPIRED BY A SUMMER TRIP TO THE FARMERS' MARKET. WHILE SHOPPING FOR VEGETABLES AT MY LOCAL FARMSTAND, I SAW SMALL RIPE FIGS—THE FIRST OF THE SEASON—AND I HAD TO BUY THEM FOR THAT NIGHT'S DINNER. I ROASTED THE FIGS IN PORT, ADDED THEM TO A MIX OF GREENS, ARUGULA, AND RADICCHIO, AND TOPPED THE SALAD WITH CRUMBLED STILTON CHEESE. I USE BLACK FIG VINEGAR, WHICH IS AVAILABLE IN SPECIALTY AND GOURMET MARKETS, IN THIS RECIPE, AND IT IS DEFINITELY WORTH SEEKING OUT. YOU CAN ALSO MAKE IT WITH RED WINE OR BALSAMIC VINEGAR, AS WELL AS WITH BLUE CHEESE INSTEAD OF STILTON.

9 small ripe figs

½ cup port

3 cups mixed salad greens

1 cup trimmed arugula, rinsed and dried

1 small head radicchio, outer leaves discarded, inner leaves torn into small pieces

VINAIGRETTE:

1 tablespoon black fig vinegar

3 tablespoons extra-virgin olive oil

Kosher salt and freshly ground black pepper

½ cup crumbled Stilton or blue cheese

1. Preheat the oven to 350°F.

2. Cut the figs in half lengthwise and trim the stems. Pour ¼ cup of the port into a nonreactive baking dish and put the figs, cut-side up, in 1 layer in the dish. Pour the remaining port over the figs. Roast the figs, occasionally spooning with the port, until softened, 30 to 35 minutes. Remove and let cool a bit.

3. Put the greens, arugula, and radicchio in a large salad bowl.

4. In a small bowl, whisk together the vinegar, olive oil, and salt and pepper to taste until well combined. Pour half of the vinaigrette over the greens and toss well.

5. Arrange the greens on individual plates, add 3 fig halves per serving, and sprinkle with the cheese. Drizzle each serving with the remaining vinaigrette and serve at once.

Serves 6

Autumn Fruit Salad with Goat Cheese & Pecans

AUTUMN FRUIT MIXED WITH GREENS, GOAT CHEESE, AND A LEMONY VINAIGRETTE MAKES A GOOD SALAD STARTER FOR A DINNER OF ROAST CHICKEN OR DUCK.

2 heads endive

2 bunches watercress, stemmed

1 cup mixed salad greens

1 red apple, cored and cut
   into 1-inch cubes

1 Granny Smith apple, cored
   and cut into 1-inch cubes

1 Bosc pear, cored and cut
   into 1-inch cubes

VINAIGRETTE:

1 tablespoon Dijon mustard

1 tablespoon white wine vinegar

1 teaspoon fresh lemon juice

1/2 cup extra-virgin olive oil

1/2 cup pecan halves, toasted
   (see page 17)

3/4 cup crumbled goat cheese

Kosher salt and freshly ground
   black pepper

1. Tear the endive leaves in half and place in a large bowl. Add the watercress, mixed greens, apples, and pear and toss to combine.

2. In a small bowl, whisk together the mustard, vinegar, and lemon juice. Slowly add the olive oil, whisking constantly, until the vinaigrette thickens.

3. Toss about 1/3 cup of the vinaigrette with the salad and heap the salad onto a platter or individual salad plates. Sprinkle the pecan halves and crumbled cheese over the top. Drizzle the salad with the remaining vinaigrette. Season to taste with salt and pepper and serve at once.

Serves 6

Apple, Cranberry & Almond Salad

THIS SALAD IS GREAT MADE WITH THE SEASON'S FIRST FRESH APPLES. LOOK FOR CRISP AND TART ONES, SUCH AS JONATHANS, MACOUNS, OR MUTSUS.

4 sweet-tart apples, cored and cut into 1-inch cubes

½ cup dried cranberries

½ cup almonds, toasted and chopped (see page 17)

2 cups shredded radicchio

2 tablespoons fresh lemon juice

VINAIGRETTE:

2 tablespoons honey mustard

6 tablespoons extra-virgin olive oil

1 tablespoon light cream

1. Put the apples, cranberries, almonds, and radicchio in a large bowl. Sprinkle with lemon juice and toss well.

2. In a small bowl, whisk together the mustard and olive oil. Add the cream and whisk again until well combined.

3. Pour the vinaigrette over the apple mixture and toss to combine. Serve the salad chilled or at room temperature.

Serves 6

BEANS

Few foods compare with dried beans when it comes to versatility, taste, and nutrition. Their flavors are neutral enough to complement a variety of other ingredients, but they can stand just as well on their own.

This chapter offers an array of recipes for all seasons. In spring and summer, serve Chickpea-Tapenade Salad or a mix of fava beans, garden-fresh tomatoes, and feta cheese. Make Warm Beans & Greens Salad when cold-weather days cry out for hearty dishes. These savory salads are delicious and very good for you as well.

Lentil, Olive & Feta Cheese Salad

Two salads are better than one! For a festive outdoor lunch, serve this with Grilled Lamb, Eggplant & Pepper Salad (page 129).

2 tablespoons olive oil

2 cloves garlic, thinly sliced

2½ cups lentils, rinsed

½ cup kalamata olives, pitted and chopped

½ cup chopped fresh flat-leaf parsley

½ cup crumbled feta cheese

Kosher salt and freshly ground black pepper

VINAIGRETTE:

1 tablespoon sherry vinegar

1 teaspoon Dijon mustard

1 tablespoon fresh lemon juice

5 tablespoons extra-virgin olive oil

1. Heat the olive oil in a large skillet or sauté pan over medium-high heat. Add the garlic and cook until softened, about 5 minutes. Add the lentils and stir well to coat. Cover with 2½ cups water. Bring to a boil, lower the heat, cover, and cook, stirring occasionally, until the lentils are tender and all of the liquid is absorbed, about 20 minutes. Drain and transfer to a large bowl.

2. Add the olives, parsley, half of the cheese, and salt and pepper to taste and toss gently to combine.

3. In a small bowl, whisk together the vinegar, mustard, and lemon juice. Slowly add the extra-virgin olive oil, whisking constantly, until the vinaigrette thickens. Pour the vinaigrette over the lentil mixture and toss well to combine. Taste and adjust the seasonings, if necessary. Sprinkle the salad with the remaining cheese and serve at room temperature.

Serves 8

Chickpea-Tapenade Salad

TAPENADE, WHICH IS A PASTE MADE WITH OLIVES AND CAPERS, IS NOW READILY AVAILABLE IN MARKETS AND SPECIALTY SHOPS. IT IS EXCELLENT WHEN MIXED WITH CRUSHED GARLIC AND OLIVE OIL AND ADDED TO SALADS, ESPECIALLY THIS ONE MADE WITH CHICKPEAS AND RED PEPPERS.

2 cups dried chickpeas

2 cups chicken broth

1 1/2 cups chopped fennel

1 red bell pepper, seeded, deveined, and diced

6 scallions, trimmed and minced

1/4 cup chopped black olives

1/2 cup chopped fresh flat-leaf parsley

3 tablespoons fresh lemon juice

VINAIGRETTE:

1 clove garlic, minced

2 tablespoons black olive tapenade

6 tablespoons extra-virgin olive oil

Freshly ground black pepper

1. Rinse the chickpeas and put in a large bowl. Cover by about 2 inches with cold water and soak for 6 to 8 hours or overnight.

2. Drain the chickpeas and put them in a large soup pot. Add the chicken broth and 4 cups water and bring to a boil over high heat. Reduce the heat and simmer the chickpeas, partially covered, until just tender, about 45 to 50 minutes. Be careful not to overcook. Drain the chickpeas and rinse them under cold water. Set aside in a large bowl to cool.

3. Add the fennel, bell pepper, scallions, olives, and parsley to the bowl. Sprinkle with 2 tablespoons of the lemon juice and toss to combine.

4. In a small bowl, combine the garlic and tapenade. Slowly whisk in the olive oil until thick.

5. Pour the vinaigrette over the chickpea mixture and toss well to combine. Add the remaining 1 tablespoon lemon juice and pepper to taste and toss again. Taste and adjust the seasonings, if necessary. Serve at room temperature.

Serves 8

Black & White Bean Salad

BLACK AND WHITE BEANS ASSUME A REFRESHING SUMMERY APPEAL WHEN TOSSED WITH RED PEPPERS AND CHIVES. IF YOU PREPARE THIS AHEAD OF TIME, REFRESH THE BEANS WITH OLIVE OIL JUST BEFORE SERVING.

1 1/2 cups dried black beans

1 1/2 cups dried navy beans

4 cups chicken broth

2 onions

2 carrots

2 ribs celery, trimmed

12 sprigs fresh flat-leaf parsley

VINAIGRETTE:

1 tablespoon Dijon mustard

2 tablespoons balsamic vinegar

2 cloves garlic, finely minced

1/2 cup extra-virgin olive oil

Kosher salt and freshly ground
   black pepper

1 red bell pepper, seeded,
   deveined, and cut into 1/4-inch
   dice

1/4 cup chopped fresh chives

1/4 cup chopped fresh flat-leaf
   parsley

Long chives, for garnish

1. Rinse the black beans and navy beans separately and put in separate bowls. Cover by about 2 inches with cold water and soak for 6 to 8 hours or overnight.

2. Drain the beans and put them in separate large soup pots. To each pot, add 2 cups chicken broth, 2 cups water, 1 onion, 1 carrot, 1 celery rib, and 6 parsley sprigs. Bring to a boil over high heat. Reduce the heat and simmer the beans until just tender, about 45 to 50 minutes. Be careful not to overcook.

3. Drain the beans, discarding the vegetables, and rinse them under cold water. Combine the beans in a large bowl and set aside to cool.

4. In a small bowl, combine the mustard, vinegar, and garlic. Slowly whisk in the olive oil until thick. Season the vinaigrette to taste with salt and pepper.

5. Add the bell pepper, chives, and chopped parsley to the beans. Toss gently. Pour the vinaigrette over the beans and toss well. Set aside for at least 1 hour to give the flavors time to blend. Or cover and refrigerate for up to 12 hours before serving. Taste and adjust the seasonings, if necessary. Garnish with long chives and serve chilled or at room temperature.

Serves 8 to 10

Black Bean & Roasted Sweet Potato Salad

BLACK BEANS AND OVEN-ROASTED SWEET POTATOES COMBINE TO MAKE THIS HEARTY AND FLAVORFUL SALAD. THIS IS A VERY GOOD DISH TO SERVE TO A HUNGRY CROWD.

2 cups dried black beans

2 cups chicken broth

1 onion

1 carrot

1 rib celery, trimmed

12 sprigs fresh flat-leaf parsley

4 sweet potatoes, peeled and cut into 1/2-inch pieces

1 tablespoon olive oil

Kosher salt

1 red onion, diced

3 tablespoons chopped fresh cilantro

3 tablespoons chopped fresh flat-leaf parsley

VINAIGRETTE:

2 tablespoons red wine vinegar

3 tablespoons orange juice

1 tablespoon fresh lime juice

1 teaspoon ground cumin

1 teaspoon chili powder

1/2 cup extra-virgin olive oil

Freshly ground black pepper

1. Rinse the beans and put in a large bowl. Cover by about 2 inches with cold water and soak for 6 to 8 hours or overnight.

2. Drain the beans and put them in a large soup pot. Add the chicken broth, 4 cups water, onion, carrot, celery, and parsley sprigs to the pot. Bring to a boil over high heat. Reduce the heat and simmer the beans until just tender, about 45 to 50 minutes. Be careful not to overcook. Drain the beans, discarding the vegetables, and rinse them under cold water. Set aside in a large bowl to cool.

3. Meanwhile, preheat the oven to 350°F. Put the sweet potatoes on a baking sheet and toss to coat with the olive oil and a bit of salt. Bake the sweet potatoes, stirring occasionally, until fork-tender, 50 minutes to 1 hour. Remove and set aside to cool.

4. Add the sweet potatoes, red onion, 2 tablespoons of the cilantro, and 2 tablespoons of the chopped parsley to the beans and toss gently to combine.

continued

5. In a small bowl, combine the vinegar, orange juice, lime juice, cumin, and chili powder. Slowly whisk in the extra-virgin olive oil until thick. Season to taste with salt and pepper.

6. Pour the vinaigrette over the bean and sweet potato mixture and toss gently to combine. Taste and adjust the seasonings, if necessary. Garnish the salad with the remaining 1 tablespoon cilantro and 1 tablespoon parsley and serve at room temperature.

Serves 8 to 10

Although it is preferable to use dried beans in these recipes, it is fine to use canned beans, especially if you are pressed for time and can't soak and boil the beans. Remember to rinse and drain canned beans well before using to get rid of the salt that is added to help preserve their shape, texture, and flavor.

Fava Bean, Tomato & Feta Cheese Salad

ALTHOUGH COOKING FRESH FAVA BEANS IS RATHER LABOR INTENSIVE, IT IS WELL WORTH THE EFFORT BECAUSE THE BEANS ADD A RICH, NUTTY FLAVOR TO ANY DISH. I LIKE TO USE THEM IN A SALAD OF RIPE RED TOMATOES, CAPERS, AND FETA CHEESE FLAVORED WITH JUST A HINT OF FRESH OREGANO.

I large ripe tomato, finely diced

1/2 red onion, finely diced

I tablespoon drained capers

5 tablespoons extra-virgin olive oil

3 pounds fresh fava beans, shelled

2 cloves garlic, thinly sliced

Kosher salt and freshly ground black pepper

6 cups mixed salad greens

3/4 cup crumbled feta cheese

I tablespoon fresh oregano leaves, crushed

1. Put the tomato, onion, capers, and 2 tablespoons of the olive oil in a large bowl. Stir well to combine and let sit for about 1/2 hour.

2. Bring a large pot of salted water to a boil. Add the beans and cook over medium-high heat until the skins wither and begin to split, about 3 minutes. Drain and transfer to a bowl of ice water. Slip the beans out of their skins.

3. Heat 2 tablespoons of the remaining olive oil in a large skillet or sauté pan over medium-high heat. Add the garlic and cook until soft, about 2 minutes. Add the beans and salt and pepper to taste and cook, stirring occasionally, until heated through, about 2 minutes.

4. Arrange the salad greens on a large platter or individual plates. Spoon the fava beans over the greens and top with the tomato mixture and its juices. Sprinkle with the cheese.

5. Whisk the remaining 1 tablespoon olive oil and the oregano together and drizzle over the cheese. Season with additional pepper and serve at once.

Serves 6

Flageolet & Vegetable Salad

TENDER, PALE-GREEN FLAGEOLETS ARE TINY FRENCH KIDNEY BEANS, AND SINCE THEY ARE GENERALLY SOLD DRIED, THEY REQUIRE OVERNIGHT SOAKING. HERE, THESE DELICATELY FLAVORED BEANS AND A MIX OF ROASTED AND STEAMED VEGETABLES ARE ACCENTUATED BY A LEMONY VINAIGRETTE. THIS SALAD CAN BE SERVED AT ROOM TEMPERATURE OR CHILLED, DEPENDING ON YOUR PREFERENCE AND YOUR TIMETABLE.

1 pound dried flageolet beans

1/2 pound carrots, sliced into 1-inch rounds

2 fennel bulbs, trimmed and quartered

2 tablespoons olive oil

Kosher salt

1 pound haricots verts, trimmed

1 pound asparagus, trimmed

1. Rinse the flageolets and put them in a large bowl. Cover by about 1 inch with cold water and soak for 6 to 8 hours or overnight.

2. Drain the flageolets and transfer them to a soup pot. Add enough salted water to cover and bring to a boil over high heat. Reduce the heat and simmer, uncovered, until just tender, about 1 hour. Drain and set aside.

3. Preheat the oven to 350°F.

4. Put the carrots and fennel in a roasting pan. Add the olive oil and salt to taste and mix well. Roast, uncovered, until tender, about 1 hour. Set aside.

5. In a saucepan or deep skillet, cook the haricots verts in water to cover until just tender, about 5 minutes. Drain and set aside. Repeat with the asparagus.

VINAIGRETTE:

¼ cup red wine vinegar

2 tablespoons fresh lemon juice

**2 tablespoons herbes
de Provence or a mixture of
dried oregano, basil, rosemary,
sage, and thyme**

½ cup extra-virgin olive oil

Freshly ground black pepper

6. In a small bowl, whisk the vinegar, lemon juice, and herbs together to combine. Slowly add the extra-virgin olive oil, whisking constantly, until well combined. Season to taste with salt and pepper.

7. Transfer the flageolets, carrot mixture, haricots verts, and asparagus to a large bowl. Pour the vinaigrette over the mixture and toss gently to combine. Season to taste with salt and pepper and serve at room temperature or chilled.

Serves 6 to 8

Warm Beans & Greens Salad

This hearty salad uses warm mixed greens as a base for cooked white beans and chopped bacon, and it is a winning dish. Many farmers' markets and high-quality supermarkets sell mixtures of dark leafy greens or braising greens, and they are well worth seeking out. Collards, turnip greens, mustard greens, spinach, Swiss chard, and kale work well in any combination in this recipe.

2 cups dried small white beans

2 cups chicken broth

4 slices bacon

2 tablespoons extra-virgin olive oil

2 cloves garlic, sliced

10 cups (about 2½ pounds) braising greens

Kosher salt and freshly ground black pepper

VINAIGRETTE:

1 teaspoon Dijon mustard

1 tablespoon white wine vinegar

2 teaspoons finely chopped shallot

6 tablespoons extra-virgin olive oil

2 tablespoons chopped fresh flat-leaf parsley

1. Rinse the beans and put in a large bowl. Cover by about 2 inches with cold water and soak for 6 to 8 hours or overnight.

2. Drain the beans and put them in a soup pot. Add the chicken broth and 4 cups water and bring to a boil over high heat. Reduce the heat and simmer the beans until just tender, about 35 to 40 minutes. Be careful not to overcook. Drain the beans; rinse them under cold water and set aside.

3. Fry the bacon in a large skillet or sauté pan until crisp and drain on paper towels. When cool enough to handle, crumble and set aside. Drain all but 1 tablespoon of bacon drippings from the pan and add the olive oil. Add the garlic and cook until just softened, about 2 minutes.

continued

4. Add the greens and cook over medium-high heat, tossing with a large spoon, spatula, or tongs. Continue cooking and tossing the greens until they are just tender and wilted, about 3 to 5 minutes. Season with salt and pepper to taste. Transfer the greens to a platter or bowl and keep warm. Add the beans and the reserved bacon to the pan and cook until warmed through, 2 to 3 minutes. Remove from the heat.

5. In a small bowl, whisk the mustard, vinegar, and shallot together. Slowly add the olive oil, whisking constantly, until well combined. Season to taste with salt and pepper. Pour the vinaigrette over the beans and mix well.

6. Arrange the warm greens on a platter or on individual plates. Spoon the beans over the greens. Garnish with parsley and serve at once.

Serves 6

Mexican-Style Red Bean Salad

BECAUSE RED KIDNEY BEANS HAVE A RATHER NEUTRAL FLAVOR, THEY CAN TAKE A LOT OF HEAT AND SPICE. SO DON'T HOLD BACK ON THE HOT SAUCE OR THE CHILI POWDER WHEN MAKING THIS DISH. THIS IS A GREAT SIDE SALAD TO SERVE WITH BARBECUED CHICKEN OR RIBS.

1 pound dried small red kidney beans

3 cups chicken broth

4 scallions, trimmed and minced

2 plum tomatoes, chopped

¼ cup chopped fresh cilantro

1 tablespoon fresh lime juice

5 or 6 dashes of hot sauce

Kosher salt and freshly ground black pepper

VINAIGRETTE:

1 tablespoon ground cumin

1 tablespoon chili powder

2 tablespoons red wine vinegar

6 tablespoons extra-virgin olive oil

½ cup freshly grated cheddar cheese

1. Rinse the beans and put in a large bowl. Cover by about 2 inches with cold water and soak for 6 to 8 hours or overnight.

2. Drain the beans and put them in a soup pot. Add the chicken broth and 3 cups water and bring to a boil over high heat. Reduce the heat and simmer the beans until just tender, about 50 to 60 minutes. Be careful not to overcook. Drain the beans; rinse them under cold water and transfer to a large bowl.

3. Add the scallions, tomatoes, cilantro, lime juice, hot sauce, and salt and pepper to taste to the beans and toss well to combine.

4. Put the cumin and chili powder in a small nonstick skillet or sauté pan and stir over medium heat until they start to smoke, about 2 to 3 minutes. Transfer to a small bowl. Add the vinegar and olive oil and whisk until well combined.

5. Pour the vinaigrette over the bean mixture and toss well. Taste and adjust the seasonings, if necessary. Sprinkle the cheese over the salad and serve at room temperature with additional hot sauce and lime, if desired.

Serves 6 to 8

GRAINS,
RICE & PASTA

The simplicity and versatility of grains, rice, and pasta allow you to become enormously creative when devising salad recipes.

These salads are easy to prepare and can be served as side dishes or main courses, depending on your time frame and your appetite. Keep your pantry stocked with a bounty of grains and rice—such as bulgur, wild rice, couscous, basmati rice, and a variety of pastas—for those moments of inspiration.

Couscous, Roasted Onion & Pepper Salad

ALTHOUGH COUSCOUS, A GRANULAR SEMOLINA, IS USUALLY SOLD IN PACKAGE FORM, IT IS JUST AS EASY TO MAKE FROM SCRATCH. IT CAN BE PURCHASED IN BULK IN HEALTH FOOD STORES AND MIDDLE EASTERN MARKETS. TRY IT WITH OVEN-ROASTED ONIONS AND BELL PEPPERS AND FRESH HERBS.

2 small red onions, halved

1 red or yellow bell pepper, seeded, deveined, and quartered

3 tablespoons olive oil

Kosher salt

1 1/2 cups couscous

2 cups chicken or vegetable broth

1/2 cup chopped fresh mint

1/2 cup chopped fresh flat-leaf parsley

VINAIGRETTE:

1 tablespoon white wine vinegar

1 tablespoon fresh lemon juice

Pinch of sugar

3 tablespoons extra-virgin olive oil

Freshly ground black pepper

1. Preheat the oven to 350°F.

2. Put the onions and pepper in a roasting pan, pour 2 tablespoons of the olive oil over them, add salt to taste, and toss to coat. Roast the vegetables until very tender, about 1 hour. Set aside. When cool enough to handle, cut into small pieces.

3. Put the couscous in a large bowl. In a small saucepan bring the broth and the remaining 1 tablespoon olive oil to a boil. Pour over the couscous and stir well. Cover the bowl with plastic wrap and let the couscous steep until it has absorbed all of the broth, about 10 minutes.

4. Fluff the couscous with a fork. Add the mint, parsley, and roasted vegetables and toss well. In a small bowl, whisk together the vinegar, lemon juice, sugar, and extra-virgin olive oil to combine. Pour over the salad and toss well to combine. Season with salt and pepper to taste. Serve at room temperature or chilled.

Serves 6

Tabbouleh Salad
with Haricots Verts & Cherry Tomatoes

TABBOULEH SALAD, MADE WITH BULGUR WHEAT AND GENEROUS AMOUNTS OF PARSLEY AND MINT, IS A REFRESHING STAPLE FOR WARM-WEATHER EATING. OTHER GOOD INGREDIENTS TO ADD TO THIS SALAD ARE CUCUMBERS, GRILLED CORN, AND DILL, DEPENDING ON YOUR TASTE AND WHAT'S ON HAND.

1 1/2 cups bulgur wheat

4 tablespoons fresh lemon juice

6 tablespoons extra-virgin
   olive oil

Kosher salt and freshly ground
   black pepper

4 scallions, trimmed and minced

1 cup chopped fresh flat-leaf
   parsley

1/2 cup chopped fresh mint

4 to 6 dashes of hot sauce
   (optional)

1/2 pound haricots verts or
   green beans, trimmed

1 bunch watercress, stemmed

8 cherry tomatoes, halved

Lemon wedges, for garnish

1. Put the bulgur in a large bowl. Pour 2 cups of boiling water over it. Cover the bowl with plastic wrap and let the bulgur steep until it has absorbed all of the water, about 30 minutes.

2. Fluff the bulgur with a fork. Add 2 tablespoons of the lemon juice, 2 tablespoons of the olive oil, and salt and pepper to taste and mix well. Add the scallions, parsley, mint, and hot sauce, if using, and toss to combine. Add the remaining 2 tablespoons lemon juice and 2 tablespoons of the olive oil and toss again. Taste and adjust the seasonings, if necessary.

3. Bring a pot of salted water to a boil. Add the beans and cook until crisp-tender, 3 to 4 minutes. Drain and cool.

4. Arrange the watercress on a large platter and spoon the bulgur mixture over it. Arrange the beans and cherry tomatoes over the top and sides of the salad. Drizzle with the remaining 2 tablespoons olive oil, garnish with lemon wedges, and serve at room temperature or chilled.

Serves 6

Herbed Barley & Mushroom Salad

BARLEY, A GRAIN OF THE GRASS FAMILY, MAKES A DELICIOUSLY CHEWY AND NUTTY-TASTING SALAD. HERE IT IS PAIRED WITH SHIITAKE AND CREMINI MUSHROOMS AND FRESH PARSLEY AND CHIVES, BUT MANY OTHER TYPES OF MUSHROOMS AND HERBS WILL WORK WELL. FOR EXTRA FLAVOR, REFRESH THE SALAD WITH A BIT MORE LEMON AND OLIVE OIL JUST BEFORE SERVING.

1 pound barley

1 cup chicken broth

3 tablespoons olive oil

2 cloves garlic, sliced

1 tablespoon minced fresh ginger

¼ pound shiitake mushrooms, sliced

¼ pound cremini mushrooms, sliced

⅓ cup sherry

Kosher salt and freshly ground black pepper

4 scallions, trimmed and minced

½ cup chopped fresh flat-leaf parsley

¼ cup minced fresh chives

VINAIGRETTE:

2 tablespoons fresh lemon juice

1 tablespoon sherry vinegar

3 tablespoons extra-virgin olive oil

1. Put the barley in a large pot and add 2 cups water and the chicken broth. Bring to a boil, reduce the heat, and simmer, covered, until the barley is tender, 30 to 40 minutes. Stir occasionally so the barley doesn't stick to the pan. Drain and cool to room temperature.

2. Heat the olive oil in a large skillet or sauté pan. Add the garlic and ginger and sauté over medium-high heat for about 2 minutes. Add the mushrooms and sauté until browned, stirring often. Add the sherry and salt and pepper to taste and continue to cook until all of the liquid is absorbed. Set aside to cool.

3. Transfer the barley and the mushrooms to a large bowl and toss together. Add the scallions, parsley, and chives and toss together.

4. In a small bowl, whisk together the lemon juice, vinegar, and extra-virgin olive oil until well combined. Pour over the barley salad and toss well to combine. Taste and adjust the seasonings, if necessary. Serve chilled or at room temperature.

Serves 6 to 8

Basmati Rice Salad with Fresh Peas, Corn & Chives

A ROOM-TEMPERATURE OR COLD RICE SALAD IS A GOOD ACCOMPANIMENT FOR MANY DISHES. THIS ONE, MADE WITH GARDEN-FRESH PEAS AND CORN, IS GREAT WITH GRILLED FISH OR ROASTED LAMB.

1½ cups basmati rice

VINAIGRETTE:

3 tablespoons white wine vinegar

1 clove garlic, minced

1 teaspoon minced fresh thyme or tarragon

¼ cup extra-virgin olive oil

Kosher salt and freshly ground black pepper

Grated zest of ½ lemon

1¼ cups cooked fresh peas

1½ cups cooked corn kernels (from 2 ears fresh corn)

¼ cup chopped fresh chives

Radicchio leaves, for serving

1. Cook the rice according to the package directions; you should have about 4 cups. Fluff with a fork and set aside to cool to room temperature.

2. In a small bowl, whisk together the vinegar, garlic, and thyme or tarragon. Add the olive oil and whisk until combined. Season to taste with salt and pepper. Cover and set aside.

3. Transfer the rice to a large bowl. Add the lemon zest, peas, corn, and chives and toss to combine. Pour the vinaigrette over the salad and toss gently until all ingredients are well mixed. Season to taste with salt and pepper. Cover and chill for 30 to 60 minutes. Let the salad return to room temperature before serving.

4. Arrange radicchio leaves on a large platter. Spoon the rice salad over them and serve.

Serves 6

Wild Rice, Apricot & Pecan Salad

THIS IS A GREAT SALAD TO SERVE AS PART OF A HOLIDAY DINNER OR BUFFET. IT GOES PARTICULARLY WELL WITH ROAST TURKEY OR HAM.

One 12-ounce package wild rice

½ cup chopped dried apricots

½ cup pecan halves, toasted (see page 17)

VINAIGRETTE:

1 teaspoon Dijon mustard

1 tablespoon red wine vinegar

3 tablespoons extra-virgin olive oil

Dash of hot sauce

Kosher salt and freshly ground black pepper

½ cup chopped fresh flat-leaf parsley

1. Cook the wild rice according to the package directions, drain and cool. Transfer the rice to a large bowl. Add the apricots and pecans and toss together.

2. In a small bowl, whisk together the mustard, vinegar, olive oil, hot sauce, and salt and pepper to taste to combine. Pour over the rice and toss together.

3. Taste and adjust the seasonings, if necessary. Garnish the salad with parsley and serve at room temperature.

Serves 6 to 8

If using bulk wild rice instead of the packaged variety, cook 1 cup of rice with 3 cups of water or chicken or vegetable broth. Bring the rice and liquid to a boil, reduce the heat, cover, and simmer, stirring occasionally, until the rice is just tender, about 40 to 50 minutes. Drain and cool.

Spicy Soba Noodle Salad

THIS DELICIOUS SALAD CAN BE SERVED IN A NUMBER OF WAYS. IT'S VERY GOOD ON ITS OWN WITH SPICY VINAIGRETTE, AS WELL AS WITH SHREDDED CHICKEN, TURKEY, OR TOFU. SOBA NOODLES, WHICH ARE MADE FROM BUCKWHEAT, CAN BE FOUND IN HEALTH FOOD STORES AND ASIAN MARKETS.

One 12-ounce package soba noodles

VINAIGRETTE:

3 tablespoons light soy sauce

3 tablespoons rice vinegar

2 tablespoons toasted sesame oil

1 tablespoon sugar

1 tablespoon hot sauce

4 scallions, trimmed and minced

1/2 cup chopped fresh flat-leaf parsley

1/2 cup sesame seeds

4 cups mixed salad greens

1. Cook the soba noodles according to the package directions. Rinse, drain, and cool. Transfer the noodles to a large bowl.

2. In a small bowl, whisk together the soy sauce, vinegar, sesame oil, sugar, and hot sauce until well combined. Pour over the noodles and toss well. Add the scallions and parsley and toss again.

3. Heat a nonstick skillet or sauté pan over low heat. Add the sesame seeds and cook, stirring often, until just golden brown, about 3 minutes. Add them to the salad and toss again. Cover and chill for up to 2 hours or overnight.

4. Arrange the mixed greens on a large platter and top with the soba noodles. Garnish with additional parsley and serve chilled or at room temperature.

Serves 6

Orzo & Roasted Vegetable Salad

THIS COLORFUL SALAD GOES WELL WITH ANY COMBINATION OF ROASTED VEGETABLES.

4 small beets, preferably a mix
of red and gold

6 tablespoons extra-virgin
olive oil

2 teaspoons balsamic vinegar

4 carrots, cut into 1/2-inch disks

4 parsnips, cut into 1/2-inch disks

6 shallots

Kosher salt

1 pound orzo pasta

3 tablespoons fresh lemon juice

8 scallions, trimmed and minced

1/2 cup chopped fresh flat-leaf
parsley

1/3 cup pine nuts, lightly toasted
(see page 17)

Freshly ground black pepper

1. Preheat the oven to 350°F.

2. Wrap the beets tightly in foil to make 2 packages (2 beets in each) and roast until tender, about 1 hour. Let cool, slip off the skins, and cut the beets into quarters lengthwise. Transfer to a medium bowl. Add 1 tablespoon of the olive oil and 1 teaspoon of the vinegar and toss together.

3. Meanwhile, put the carrots, parsnips, and shallots in a large roasting pan. Add 2 tablespoons of the olive oil and salt to taste and toss well to coat the vegetables. Roast, stirring occasionally, until the vegetables are lightly browned and tender, about 30 to 40 minutes. Transfer to a medium bowl. Add the remaining 1 teaspoon vinegar and 1 tablespoon of the olive oil and toss together.

4. Cook the orzo according to the package directions. Drain, cool, and transfer to a large bowl. Add 2 tablespoons of the lemon juice and toss well. Stir in the roasted carrot mixture, scallions, parsley, and pine nuts and toss gently to combine. Add the remaining 1 tablespoon lemon juice, the remaining 2 tablespoons olive oil, and salt and pepper to taste and toss well. Spoon the reserved beets over the top of the salad. Drizzle with additional lemon juice and olive oil, if desired, and serve at room temperature.

Serves 6 to 8

Orecchiette, Tomato & Zucchini Salad

ORECCHIETTE, WHICH LITERALLY MEANS "LITTLE EARS," IS A FABULOUS PASTA TO MIX WITH CHOPPED FRESH TOMATOES AND BASIL AND SAUTÉED ONION AND ZUCCHINI. THE MIX OF BOTH RAW AND COOKED VEGETABLES WITH PASTA IS VERY INTERESTING, AND IT MAKES A SUBSTANTIAL MAIN-COURSE SALAD.

1 pound orecchiette pasta

2 ripe tomatoes, cut into
   1-inch pieces

2 tablespoons chopped fresh
   basil

3 tablespoons extra-virgin
   olive oil

1/2 red onion, finely diced

1 zucchini, peeled and finely
   diced

Kosher salt and freshly ground
   black pepper

1 tablespoon red wine vinegar

1/2 cup kalamata olives, pitted
   and halved

1. Bring a large pot of salted water to a boil, add the pasta, and cook according to the package directions. Drain and set aside.

2. Meanwhile, put the tomatoes and basil in a large bowl, toss together, and set aside.

3. Heat 1 tablespoon of the olive oil in a skillet or sauté pan and cook the onion and zucchini over medium heat until tender and golden brown, 5 to 7 minutes. Add the zucchini mixture to the tomatoes and basil and toss well to combine. Season to taste with salt and pepper.

4. In a small bowl, whisk together the vinegar and the remaining 2 tablespoons olive oil until well combined. Pour the vinaigrette over the pasta and toss. Add the tomato-zucchini mixture and the olives to the pasta and toss well to combine. Taste and adjust the seasonings, if necessary, and serve.

Serves 6 to 8

Penne & Green Beans with Parsley-Pecan Pesto Sauce

THIS PASTA SALAD IS ONE OF MY FAMILY'S FAVORITE RECIPES. IT IS A DELICIOUS COMBINATION OF PENNE, GREEN BEANS, AND PESTO SAUCE MADE WITH FRESH PARSLEY AND BASIL JUST PICKED FROM THE GARDEN. PERFECT FOR A HOT SUMMER EVENING.

½ cup pecan halves

¾ cup fresh flat-leaf parsley leaves

¾ cup fresh basil leaves

2 cloves garlic, sliced

1 tablespoon fresh lemon juice

¾ cup extra-virgin olive oil

Kosher salt and freshly ground black pepper

1 pound penne pasta

¾ pound green beans, trimmed

Freshly grated Parmesan cheese, for serving

1. Put the pecans, parsley, basil, garlic, and lemon juice in a food processor and pulse until well blended. With the motor running, slowly add the olive oil until well blended. Season with salt and pepper to taste. The pesto sauce will keep, covered, in the refrigerator for up to 1 day. Bring to room temperature before using.

2. Bring a large pot of salted water to a boil, add the pasta, and cook according to the package directions. Drain and set aside.

3. Bring a medium pot of salted water to a boil, add the beans, and cook until crisp-tender, about 2 minutes. Drain and set aside.

4. Put the pasta and beans in a large bowl and toss together. Stir in the pesto and toss until well combined. Taste and adjust the seasonings, if necessary. Serve warm, chilled, or at room temperature with the cheese.

Serves 6

SEAFOOD

When considering seafood salads, we've come a long way from mixing canned tuna and mayonnaise together. Because fresh fish and shellfish are readily available from local fish shops as well as larger markets, the possibilities for making great-tasting seafood salads are endless.

This chapter has a range of recipes using the freshest seafood and produce on the market. They make impressive appetizers and entrées and are meant to be savored, like the sea itself.

Crab, Mango & Tomato Salad

THIS IS A VERY SPECIAL SALAD THAT I LIKE TO SERVE AS A LIGHT SEAFOOD STARTER. FRESH TOMATOES AND MANGOES COMPLEMENT THE CRABMEAT BEAUTIFULLY.

**1 pound lump crabmeat,
   picked over**

1/2 cup mayonnaise

2 teaspoons fresh lemon juice

1/2 teaspoon cayenne pepper

**Kosher salt and freshly ground
   black pepper**

**2 cups shredded Chinese
   or napa cabbage**

1/2 red onion, thinly sliced

VINAIGRETTE:

1 teaspoon red wine vinegar

**2 tablespoons extra-virgin
   olive oil**

1 tomato, cut into thin slices

**1 mango, peeled, pitted,
   and cut into thin slices**

**Extra-virgin olive oil,
   for drizzling**

**1/4 cup chopped fresh flat-leaf
   parsley, for garnish**

Lemon wedges, for garnish

Hot sauce (optional), for serving

1. Put the crabmeat in a large bowl. In a medium bowl, mix together the mayonnaise, lemon juice, cayenne pepper, and salt and pepper to taste. Fold into the crabmeat and mix together gently but thoroughly. The crab mixture will keep, covered, in the refrigerator for up to 6 hours.

2. Put the cabbage and onion in a large bowl. Whisk together the vinegar and olive oil until well blended. Pour over the cabbage mixture and toss.

3. Arrange the cabbage mixture on a large platter or among individual plates. Arrange the tomato and mango slices over the cabbage, drizzle with olive oil, and season with salt and pepper, if desired. Top with the crabmeat and garnish with parsley and lemon wedges. Serve at once with hot sauce, if desired.

Serves 6

Soft-Shell Crab & Fennel Salad

SOFT-SHELL CRABS, IN SEASON FROM APRIL TO SEPTEMBER, ARE ALWAYS A TREAT. THIS IS A SUREFIRE METHOD FOR FRYING SOFT-SHELLS—THEY'RE ALWAYS LIGHT, NEVER GREASY, AND UTTERLY DELICIOUS.

2 cups buttermilk

2 eggs

6 medium soft-shell crabs, cleaned

1 cup self-rising cake flour, such as Presto

1 cup yellow cornmeal

Kosher salt and freshly ground black pepper

About ¹⁄₂ cup safflower oil, for frying

4 cups mixed salad greens

1 fennel bulb, trimmed and very thinly sliced

VINAIGRETTE:

2 tablespoons white wine vinegar

1 tablespoon fresh lemon juice

1 teaspoon Dijon mustard

2 teaspoons finely chopped shallot

6 tablespoons extra-virgin olive oil

1. Whisk the buttermilk and eggs together and pour into a large shallow dish. Add the crabs and soak, covered, in the refrigerator for 1 to 2 hours.

2. Whisk together the flour, cornmeal, and salt and pepper to taste and transfer to a large plastic bag. Lift 1 crab out of the buttermilk, letting excess drip off, and shake in the bag to coat with the flour and cornmeal mixture. Shake off the excess flour and transfer to a plate. Repeat with the remaining crabs.

3. Heat the safflower oil in a skillet or sauté pan to a depth of about ¹⁄₂ inch. Fry the crabs, shell-side down, 2 or 3 at a time, until golden brown, 3 to 5 minutes. Turn and fry until crisp on the other side, about 3 minutes. Watch out for popping. Repeat with the remaining crabs, adding more oil, if necessary. Drain the crabs on paper towels.

4. Put the greens and fennel in a large bowl. Whisk together the vinegar, lemon juice, mustard, and shallot. Slowly add the olive oil, whisking constantly, until well combined. Season to taste with salt and pepper. Add half of the vinaigrette to the salad and toss well.

5. Arrange the salad on individual plates. Top each salad with a crab and drizzle each serving with the remaining vinaigrette.

Serves 6

Snapper & Avocado Ceviche Salad

CEVICHE, A DISH OF FISH OR SHELLFISH THAT "COOKS" WHILE IT MARINATES IN CITRUS JUICE, MAKES AN EXCELLENT FIRST-COURSE SALAD. PREPARE THIS WITH THE FRESHEST SNAPPER YOU CAN FIND AND HAVE YOUR FISHMONGER FILLET AND SKIN THE FISH FOR YOU. THIS CEVICHE IS ALSO VERY GOOD TO SERVE AS AN HORS D'OEUVRE WITH TORTILLA CHIPS OR GRILLED BREAD.

1 pound red snapper fillets,
   skinned and cut into
   1/4-inch cubes

1/2 cup fresh lemon juice

1/2 cup fresh lime juice

1/2 cup diced onion

1/2 cup diced red or yellow
   bell pepper

1/2 cup diced green bell pepper

1 jalapeño pepper, seeded,
   deveined, and minced

1/2 cup diced plum tomato

1 tablespoon drained capers

1/4 cup chopped green olives

2 tablespoons chopped fresh
   flat-leaf parsley

Dash of hot sauce

1 teaspoon extra-virgin olive oil

Kosher salt and freshly ground
   black pepper

2 avocados, pitted, peeled,
   and cut into 1/4-inch cubes

Romaine lettuce leaves,
   for serving

1. Put the cubed fish in a nonreactive bowl and pour the lemon and lime juices over it. Mix well, cover, and marinate in the refrigerator for about 6 hours. Stir occasionally.

2. Combine the onion, bell peppers, jalapeño, tomato, capers, olives, parsley, hot sauce, olive oil, and salt and pepper to taste and mix together. Cover and refrigerate for about 6 hours.

3. Just before serving, drain the fish, discarding the liquid, and transfer to a large bowl. Add the pepper mixture and the avocado to the fish and mix well. Taste and adjust the seasonings, if necessary.

4. Arrange the lettuce leaves in shallow soup bowls or on plates. Spoon the ceviche over the lettuce and serve at once.

Serves 6

Scallop, Shrimp & Mussel Salad

WHEN YOU'RE IN THE MOOD FOR A TASTE OF THE SEA, MAKE THIS FANTASTIC SALAD WITH FRESH SCALLOPS, SHRIMP, MUSSELS, AND BASIL VINAIGRETTE. THIS IS SEASONAL EATING AT ITS BEST.

VINAIGRETTE:

1 tablespoon white wine vinegar

1 teaspoon grated lemon zest

1 tablespoon fresh lemon juice

2 tablespoons chopped fresh basil

1 teaspoon drained capers

1/2 cup extra-virgin olive oil

Kosher salt and freshly ground black pepper

3 cups dry white wine

2 cloves garlic, thinly sliced

1 onion, chopped

2 pounds mussels, scrubbed and rinsed

1 pound bay or sea scallops (see Note on page 104)

1 pound medium shrimp (about 32 to 36 per pound)

2 ribs celery, chopped

1 small head Chinese or napa cabbage

1/2 red onion, thinly sliced

1/4 cup chopped fresh basil

1. In a small bowl, whisk together the vinegar, lemon zest, lemon juice, 2 tablespoons basil, and capers. Slowly add the olive oil, whisking constantly, until well combined. Season to taste with salt and pepper and set aside.

2. Put the wine, garlic, and chopped onion in a large soup pot. Bring to a boil, add the mussels, cover, reduce the heat to medium, and let the mussels steam until they open, about 5 minutes. (Discard any that do not open.) Remove from the heat. Transfer the mussels to a bowl with a slotted spoon and reserve the cooking liquid. Strain the liquid through cheesecloth. There should be about 3 cups.

3. Return the liquid to the soup pot and add the scallops. Bring to a boil, reduce the heat, and simmer, uncovered, for 1 minute. Add the shrimp and simmer until they turn pink and are cooked through, about 2 minutes. Drain and cool. Peel the shrimp, if desired. Transfer the scallops and shrimp to a large bowl.

continued

4. Meanwhile, remove the mussels from the shells. Add the mussels and celery to the shrimp and scallops and toss gently to combine. Pour about half of the vinaigrette over the seafood and toss again. Cover and chill for 1 hour before serving.

5. Toss the cabbage and sliced onion with the remaining vinaigrette and arrange on a large platter or individual salad plates. Spoon the seafood over it. Garnish with $\frac{1}{4}$ cup basil and serve.

Serves 6

Note: If using sea scallops, cut them in half.

Mussels signal freshness with their shells. If they are open and don't close tightly after a quick tap, that means they are unfit to eat. Check mussels after they're cooked and discard any that do not open.

Shrimp & Asparagus Salad

SHRIMP AND ASPARAGUS ARE A DELICIOUS COMBINATION AND MAKE AN EXCELLENT SALAD. BECAUSE THE COMPONENTS CAN BE MADE WELL AHEAD OF TIME AND TOSSED TOGETHER AT THE LAST MINUTE, IT'S JUST THE RIGHT THING TO SERVE FOR A CASUAL WARM-WEATHER DINNER.

1½ pounds medium shrimp
  (about 32 to 36 per pound)
1½ pounds asparagus,
  trimmed and cut into
  2-inch pieces

VINAIGRETTE:
1 tablespoon minced shallot
1 tablespoon champagne vinegar
1 tablespoon mayonnaise
1 teaspoon Dijon mustard
Pinch of sugar
Pinch of cayenne pepper
3 tablespoons peanut oil
Kosher salt and freshly ground
  black pepper

3 tablespoons pine nuts, toasted
  (see page 17)
3 scallions, trimmed and minced

1. Bring a large pot of salted water to a boil. Add the shrimp and boil until they turn pink and are cooked through, about 3 minutes. Drain the shrimp, run under cool water, and peel and devein them.

2. Bring a medium saucepan of salted water to a boil. Add the asparagus and cook over medium heat until just crisp-tender, 4 to 5 minutes. Drain and cool. The shrimp and asparagus can be prepared up to this point and chilled for up to 6 hours until ready to serve the salad.

3. In a small bowl, whisk together the shallot, vinegar, mayonnaise, mustard, sugar, and cayenne pepper. Add the peanut oil and salt and pepper to taste and whisk until well combined.

4. Put the shrimp and asparagus in a large bowl. Pour the vinaigrette over them and toss well. Taste and adjust the seasonings, if necessary.

5. Arrange the salad on a platter, garnish with pine nuts and scallions, and serve.

Serves 6

Shrimp, Fennel & White Bean Salad

THIS SALAD, LACED WITH FRESH TARRAGON VINAIGRETTE, IS A GOOD THING TO SERVE AS AN APPETIZER SALAD OR AS PART OF A BUFFET LUNCH OR DINNER.

1 cup dried navy beans

4 sprigs fresh thyme

2 bay leaves

2 cloves garlic

1 pound large shrimp
(about 32 to 36 per pound)

1/2 cup thinly sliced red onion

1 small fennel bulb, trimmed
and thinly sliced

Kosher salt and freshly ground
black pepper

VINAIGRETTE:

1 tablespoon sherry vinegar

3 tablespoons extra-virgin
olive oil

1 tablespoon chopped fresh
tarragon

Tarragon leaves, for garnish

Lemon wedges, for garnish

1. Rinse the beans and put in a large bowl. Cover by about 2 inches with cold water and soak for 6 to 8 hours or overnight.

2. Drain the beans and put them in a large soup pot. Add the thyme, bay leaves, garlic, and enough water to cover by 1 inch and bring to a boil over high heat. Reduce the heat and cook the beans at a bare simmer until just tender, 35 to 45 minutes. Be careful not to overcook. Drain the beans and rinse them under cold water. Discard the thyme sprigs, bay leaves, and garlic. Set aside in a large bowl to cool.

3. Meanwhile, bring a large pot of salted water to a boil. Add shrimp and cook for 3 to 4 minutes, until just cooked through. Drain, run under cool water, and peel and devein shrimp.

4. Add the shrimp, onion, fennel, and salt and pepper to taste to the beans and toss together.

5. In a small bowl, whisk the vinegar and olive oil together. Add the tarragon and salt and pepper to taste and whisk again until well combined. Pour over the salad and toss again. Taste and adjust the seasonings, if necessary. Served chilled or at room temperature garnished with tarragon leaves and lemon wedges.

Serves 6

Lobster, Tomato & Corn Salad

THIS SALAD IS A TRULY INDULGENT TREAT. IT INCORPORATES THE BEST INGREDIENTS OF SUMMER—
FRESH LOBSTER, TOMATOES, AND CORN.

6 cups cooked lobster meat
(see Note)

4 cups cooked corn kernels
(from 4 ears fresh corn)

3 ripe tomatoes, coarsely
chopped

3 ribs celery, diced

½ cup chopped fresh flat-leaf
parsley

3 tablespoons chopped fresh
basil

VINAIGRETTE:

2 tablespoons champagne
vinegar

5 tablespoons extra-virgin
olive oil

Kosher salt and freshly ground
black pepper

4 cups mixed salad greens,
for serving

1. Put the lobster, corn, tomatoes, celery, parsley, and basil in a large bowl and gently toss together.

2. In a small bowl, whisk together the vinegar and olive oil to combine. Pour the vinaigrette over the lobster mixture and toss gently to combine. Season to taste with salt and pepper. Taste and adjust the seasonings, if necessary. Cover and chill the salad for up to but no longer than 2 hours before serving.

3. Arrange the salad greens on a large platter. Spoon the salad over the greens and serve at once.

Serves 6

Note: A 1- to 1¼-pound lobster will yield about 1 cup of cooked lobster meat. When buying lobster for making salad or lobster rolls, look for culls (one-clawed lobsters); they are usually less expensive.

Tuna Sashimi Salad

THE KEY INGREDIENT IN THIS SALAD IS "SUSHI-QUALITY" TUNA, WHICH IS THE BEST AND FRESHEST YOU CAN BUY. YOU MAY HAVE TO SEARCH FOR A MARKET THAT SELLS IT AND IT MAY COST MORE THAN REGULAR TUNA, BUT THE RESULTS ARE WELL WORTH IT. CHOP THE TUNA ON A PRISTINE WORK SURFACE WITH A CLEAN KNIFE, TOSS IT WITH THE OTHER INGREDIENTS, AND LET IT MELLOW IN THE REFRIGERATOR FOR NO MORE THAN 2 HOURS. THE TUNA'S TEXTURE WILL SOFTEN IF YOU LET IT SIT ANY LONGER. THIS IS A VERY REFRESHING AND ELEGANT FIRST-COURSE SALAD.

1 1/2 pounds sushi-quality tuna

3 tablespoons chopped fresh cilantro

2 tablespoons minced shallot

1 teaspoon minced fresh ginger

3 tablespoons drained capers

2 teaspoons plus 5 tablespoons extra-virgin olive oil

Kosher salt and freshly ground black pepper

6 cups mixed salad greens

3 cucumbers, peeled, seeded, and cut into 1 1/2-inch julienne

1 small red onion, sliced paper thin

2 tablespoons balsamic vinegar

2 tablespoons fresh lime juice

1. Using a very sharp knife, dice the tuna as finely as possible. Transfer to a medium bowl and add the cilantro, shallot, ginger, capers, and 2 teaspoons of the olive oil. Mix gently until well combined and season to taste with salt and pepper. Cover and chill for up to but no longer than 2 hours.

2. Put the salad greens, cucumbers, and onion in a large bowl. Whisk together the vinegar and the remaining 5 tablespoons olive oil until well combined. Pour over the greens and toss to coat.

3. Gently toss the lime juice with the tuna. Arrange the salad on individual plates. Spoon the tuna over the salad and drizzle each serving with a bit of extra lime juice, if desired. Serve at once.

Serves 6

Poached Salmon & Corn Salad

THE VINAIGRETTE IN THIS RECIPE IS FABULOUS OVER POACHED SALMON AND FRESH CORN. I ALWAYS MAKE A GENEROUS AMOUNT AND KEEP IT ON HAND IN THE REFRIGERATOR BECAUSE IT ALSO GOES WELL WITH OTHER FISH, CHICKEN, AND VEGETABLES.

4 boneless salmon steaks (about 6 ounces each)

3 tablespoons white vinegar

1 cup thinly sliced onion

½ cup thinly sliced carrots

6 sprigs fresh flat-leaf parsley

3 cloves

6 black peppercorns

Kosher salt

3 cups cooked corn kernels (from 4 ears fresh corn)

1. Put the salmon steaks in a large, shallow saucepan and cover with cold water. Add the 3 tablespoons vinegar, onion, carrots, parsley sprigs, cloves, peppercorns, and salt to taste to the pan. Bring to a boil, lower the heat, and simmer, uncovered, for about 3 minutes for a pink center. If desired, poach a bit longer, but do not overcook. Remove the steaks from the poaching liquid with a slotted spoon and drain. Set aside and let cool.

2. Put the salmon in a bowl and flake it, using a fork or your fingers, discarding any small salmon bones. Add the corn and gently toss to combine.

2 teaspoons Dijon mustard

2 tablespoons drained capers

**2 tablespoons chopped fresh
flat-leaf parsley**

**2 tablespoons chopped fresh
basil**

1 tablespoon white vinegar

1 tablespoon fresh lemon juice

Freshly ground black pepper

½ cup corn or safflower oil

½ cup extra-virgin olive oil

**Romaine or Boston lettuce
leaves**

**12 cherry tomatoes, halved,
for garnish**

3. Put the mustard, capers, chopped parsley, basil, vinegar, lemon juice, and salt and pepper to taste in a food processor. Pulse 4 or 5 times. With the machine running, add the oils in a thin stream until they are well incorporated. Taste and adjust the seasonings, if necessary.

4. Pour about half of the vinaigrette into the salmon and corn mixture and toss gently to combine. Cover and chill the salad for 1 to 2 hours before serving.

5. Arrange the lettuce leaves on a large platter or on individual salad plates. Spoon the salad over the lettuce and drizzle with additional vinaigrette. Garnish with cherry tomato halves and serve.

Serves 6

POULTRY
& MEAT

These salads, which make excellent one-dish meals, incorporate poultry or meat, crisp greens, and fresh fruit and vegetables, as well as beans and nuts.

This chapter demonstrates the great versatility of salads in general. Whether you're serving Chicken, Watercress & Walnut Salad for a light lunch or presenting hearty barbecue fare like Grilled Sirloin Steak Salad with Tomatoes, Basil & Capers, they are all delicious entrée dishes that you will enjoy making for all occasions.

Chicken, Watercress & Walnut Salad

THIS IS ONE OF MY FAVORITE WAYS TO SERVE CHICKEN SALAD. I LIKE TO POACH CHICKEN BREASTS IN VEGETABLE BROTH AND LET THEM COOL IN IT AFTER THEY'RE COOKED THROUGH.

½ cup dry white wine

1 onion

2 carrots

2 ribs celery, trimmed
  and halved

12 sprigs fresh flat-leaf parsley

12 black peppercorns

Kosher salt

3 whole chicken breasts
  (about 3 pounds), split

½ cup walnut halves, toasted
  (see page 17)

VINAIGRETTE:

1 tablespoon Dijon mustard

1 tablespoon white wine vinegar

1 teaspoon sugar

⅓ cup extra-virgin olive oil

Freshly ground black pepper

1 bunch watercress, stemmed

1 to 2 tablespoons walnut oil,
  for drizzling

1. Put the wine, onion, carrots, celery, and parsley in a large soup pot. Add about 4 quarts water, the peppercorns, and salt to taste. Bring to a boil, reduce the heat, and simmer, uncovered, for 15 minutes.

2. Add the chicken breasts to the simmering broth, raise the heat, and return to a boil. Reduce the heat and gently simmer, partially covered, until the chicken is cooked through, about 25 to 30 minutes. Remove the pot from the heat and let the chicken cool in the broth.

3. Remove the chicken from the broth. Strain the broth and reserve for another use. Tear the chicken into bite-sized pieces, discarding the skin and bones, and put in a large bowl. Add the walnuts.

4. In a small bowl, whisk together the mustard, vinegar, and sugar. Slowly add the olive oil, whisking constantly, until the vinaigrette thickens. Pour over the chicken and walnuts and gently toss together until well mixed. Season with salt and pepper to taste.

5. Arrange the watercress on a large platter and spoon the chicken salad over it. Drizzle with walnut oil and serve at room temperature.

Serves 6

Chicken, Haricots Verts & Tahini Salad

TAHINI, MIDDLE EASTERN SESAME PASTE, ADDS A NICE NUTTY FLAVOR TO THE CHICKEN AND HARICOTS VERTS IN THIS SALAD. BE SURE THAT IT IS WELL STIRRED BEFORE BLENDING IT WITH THE OTHER DRESSING INGREDIENTS. THIS DRESSING IS ALSO VERY GOOD DRIZZLED OVER MIXED GREENS AND GRAINS.

$\frac{1}{2}$ **cup dry white wine**

1 onion

2 carrots

**2 ribs celery, trimmed
and halved**

12 sprigs fresh flat-leaf parsley

12 black peppercorns

Kosher salt

**3 whole chicken breasts
(about 3 pounds), split**

$\frac{1}{2}$ **pound haricots verts
or green beans, trimmed**

1. Put the wine, onion, carrots, celery, and parsley in a large soup pot. Add about 4 quarts water, the peppercorns, and salt to taste. Bring to a boil, reduce the heat, and simmer, uncovered, for 15 minutes.

2. Add the chicken breasts to the simmering broth, raise the heat, and return to a boil. Reduce the heat and gently simmer, partially covered, until the chicken is cooked through, about 25 to 30 minutes. Remove the pot from the heat and let the chicken cool in the broth.

3. Remove the chicken from the broth. Strain the broth and reserve for another use. Tear the chicken into bite-sized pieces, discarding the skin and bones, and put in a large bowl.

4. Bring a medium saucepan of salted water to a boil. Add the beans, bring back to a boil, and cook over medium heat until just crisp-tender, 4 to 5 minutes. Drain and add the beans to the chicken.

DRESSING:

2/3 cup well-stirred tahini

3 tablespoons fresh lemon juice

1 teaspoon light soy sauce

1 clove garlic, halved

Pinch of sugar

Freshly ground black pepper

Dash of hot sauce (optional)

1/2 cup cherry tomatoes, halved, for garnish

1/4 cup kalamata olives, pitted and chopped, for garnish

5. In a blender, combine the tahini, lemon juice, soy sauce, garlic, sugar, salt and pepper to taste, and hot sauce, if using, and blend until very smooth. Taste and adjust the seasonings, if necessary.

6. Pour the dressing over the chicken and beans and toss gently to coat. Arrange the salad on a platter, garnish with the tomatoes and olives, and serve.

Serves 6

To make sure that the chicken you use in salads is always moist and flavorful, try this surefire poaching method. Put some white wine, an onion, carrots, celery, and parsley in a large pot. Add about 4 quarts of water, peppercorns, and salt to taste. Bring to a boil and simmer for about 15 minutes. Add a whole unskinned chicken or chicken breasts, bring to a boil, then simmer for about 30 minutes. Let the chicken cool in the broth. Tear the chicken meat into bite-sized pieces, discarding the skin and bones. Strain the liquid and reserve for a wonderfully flavored chicken broth.

Grilled Chicken, Black Bean, Corn & Avocado Salad

THIS IS A FANTASTIC MAIN-COURSE SALAD MADE WITH CITRUS-GRILLED CHICKEN. FOR TASTIEST RESULTS, GRILL OR BROIL CHICKEN BREASTS WITH THEIR SKIN UNTIL THEY ARE NICELY CHARRED AND CRISPY.

3 whole chicken breasts (about 3 pounds), split

MARINADE:
Juice of 2 lemons

Juice of 2 limes

2 cloves garlic, thinly sliced

1 tablespoon ground cumin

¼ cup olive oil

1½ cups cooked corn kernels (from 2 ears fresh corn)

1 tomato, cut into ½-inch pieces

2 avocados, pitted, peeled, and cut into ½-inch pieces

1 cup canned black beans, drained and rinsed

4 scallions, trimmed and minced

2 tablespoons chopped fresh cilantro

Kosher salt and freshly ground black pepper

1. Put the chicken in a large nonreactive baking dish. Combine the lemon juice, lime juice, garlic, and 1 tablespoon cumin in a medium bowl. Slowly whisk in the olive oil to combine. Pour over the chicken and refrigerate for up to 8 hours or overnight, turning occasionally.

2. Prepare a gas or charcoal grill (coals are covered with a light coating of ash and glow deep red) or preheat the broiler.

3. Remove the chicken from the marinade and grill over medium-hot heat or broil about 6 to 9 inches from the heat until nicely browned and the juices run clear when pricked with a fork, about 15 minutes per side. Baste the chicken often with the marinade during grilling or broiling.

4. Remove the chicken from the heat and set aside to cool slightly. (Discard any remaining marinade.) When cool enough to handle, remove the meat from the bones and tear into pieces about 1½ inches long.

5. Put the chicken in a large bowl. Add the corn, half of the tomato pieces, half of the avocado pieces, beans, scallions, cilantro, and salt and pepper to taste and toss well.

continued

VINAIGRETTE:

1 tablespoon white vinegar

1 teaspoon ground cumin

3 tablespoons extra-virgin olive oil

4 cups mixed salad greens

Cilantro leaves, for garnish

6. In a small bowl, whisk together the vinegar and 1 teaspoon cumin. Add the extra-virgin olive oil and whisk until well combined. Pour over the chicken mixture and gently toss. Taste and adjust the seasonings, if necessary.

7. Arrange the salad greens on a large platter. Spoon the chicken salad over the greens. Garnish with the remaining tomatoes and avocados and the cilantro leaves. Serve at once.

Serves 6

Seared Duck, Orange & Olive Salad

DUCK BREASTS INFUSED WITH RED WINE AND ORANGES ARE NOT ONLY DELICIOUS BUT ALSO QUICK AND EASY TO COOK ON THE STOVETOP. THEY MAKE A SAVORY AND SUMPTUOUS MAIN-COURSE SALAD.

2 duck breasts (1 pound each)

MARINADE:
1 cup dry red wine

1 tablespoon light soy sauce

1 tablespoon hot chili sauce with garlic

Juice of 1 orange

3 tablespoons chopped orange peel

1 tablespoon olive oil

2 cloves garlic, thinly sliced

3 oranges, peeled and cut into bite-sized pieces

½ red onion, thinly sliced

16 Niçoise olives

DRESSING:
1 tablespoon Dijon mustard

2 tablespoons balsamic vinegar

¼ cup fresh orange juice

4 cups mixed salad greens

1. Put the duck breasts in a large freezer bag. In a medium bowl, whisk together the wine, soy sauce, chili sauce, and orange juice. Stir in the orange peel. Pour the marinade over the duck, seal, and marinate in the refrigerator for 6 hours or overnight.

2. Heat the olive oil in a large heavy skillet or sauté pan, add the garlic, and cook over medium heat until softened, about 2 minutes. Remove the duck from the marinade, shake off excess liquid, and and discard the marinade. Add duck to the pan and sauté, turning frequently, until cooked through, about 15 minutes. Remove the breasts from the pan and let them rest on a cutting board for 10 minutes. Put the orange pieces, onion, and olives in a bowl. Toss together and set aside.

3. Pour the fat from the pan and wipe out the pan with paper towels. Whisk together the mustard, vinegar, and ¼ cup orange juice until well blended. Add the dressing to the pan and cook over medium heat until reduced by half, stirring constantly, about 2 to 3 minutes. Remove from the heat.

4. Arrange the greens on a large platter or on individual plates. Thinly slice the duck on the diagonal and arrange over the greens. Spoon the orange mixture over the duck and pour the warm dressing over the salad. Serve at once.

Serves 6

Smoked Turkey, Grape & Pecan Salad

THIS EXCELLENT MAIN-COURSE SALAD IS LOADED WITH TEXTURE AND CRUNCH. IT IS ALSO VERY GOOD WHEN MADE WITH SMOKED HAM OR CHICKEN. BE SURE TO USE THE BEST-QUALITY SHERRY VINEGAR YOU CAN FIND FOR THE VINAIGRETTE.

3/4 pound smoked turkey,
  about 1/2 inch thick, cut into
  2-inch julienne
1 cup green seedless grapes,
  halved
1 cup red seedless grapes, halved
1/2 cup pecans, toasted
  (see page 17)
6 cups mixed salad greens

VINAIGRETTE:
1 tablespoon Dijon mustard
2 tablespoons sherry vinegar
1/3 cup extra-virgin olive oil
Freshly ground black pepper

1. Put the turkey, grapes, and half of the pecans in a large bowl and gently toss together. Put the greens in a separate large bowl.

2. In a small bowl, whisk together the mustard and vinegar. Slowly add the olive oil, whisking constantly, until well combined. Season to taste with pepper.

3. Pour half of the vinaigrette over the turkey and grape mixture and toss gently to mix well. (The turkey and grape mixture can be prepared and chilled for a few hours up to this point.)

4. Pour the remaining vinaigrette over the salad greens and toss. Arrange the salad greens on a large platter or individual plates and top with the turkey and grape mixture. Garnish with the remaining pecans and serve.

Serves 6

Grilled Pork & Mango Salad with Warm Asian Greens

SAUTÉED BOK CHOY AND BABY SPINACH TASTE FANTASTIC WITH GRILLED PORK AND MANGO. THIS IS A GREAT SALAD FOR CASUAL SUMMER DINING.

MARINADE:

¼ cup fresh mint leaves

¼ cup fresh cilantro leaves

2 tablespoons fresh basil leaves

2 cloves garlic, thinly sliced

1 jalapeño pepper, seeded
   and diced

1 tablespoon brown sugar

½ cup fresh lime juice

2 tablespoons light soy sauce

2 tablespoons fish sauce
   (nam pla)

2 tablespoons corn or
   safflower oil

2 pounds center-cut boneless
   pork cutlets or chops, about
   ½ inch thick

1 ripe mango, peeled, pitted,
   and thickly sliced

1. In a food processor, combine the mint, cilantro, basil, garlic, pepper, sugar, lime juice, 2 tablespoons soy sauce, fish sauce, and 2 tablespoons corn or safflower oil and pulse until well combined. The marinade can be made up to 1 day ahead of time.

2. Put the pork in a shallow nonreactive pan. Pour the marinade over the pork. Cover and refrigerate for 4 to 6 hours, turning occasionally.

3. Prepare a gas or charcoal grill. When it's medium-hot (coals are covered with a light coating of ash and glow deep red), grill the pork, 4 to 5 minutes per side, for medium-rare, or until desired doneness. At the same time, grill the mango slices until lightly browned, about 5 minutes. Let the pork and mango cool for a few minutes. Cut the pork into ¼-inch slices and dice the mango; set aside.

**2 tablespoons corn or
  safflower oil**

**1 head bok choy, trimmed
  and coarsely chopped**

½ pound baby spinach leaves

2 tablespoons light soy sauce

1 tablespoon toasted sesame oil

Dash of hot sauce

**4 scallions, trimmed
  and minced, for garnish**

4. Meanwhile, heat 2 tablespoons corn or safflower oil in a large skillet or sauté pan. Add the bok choy and stir-fry over medium-high heat until just tender, about 3 minutes. Add the spinach to the pan and stir-fry until just wilted, 1 to 2 minutes. Transfer the greens to a large platter or individual plates. Top the greens with the pork slices and diced mango.

5. In a small bowl, whisk together the 2 tablespoons soy sauce, sesame oil, and hot sauce. Drizzle over the pork and mango. Garnish with scallions and serve at once.

Serves 6

Thai-Style Beef & Mint Salad

FRESH MINT, THE QUINTESSENTIAL COOL FLAVOR, IS AN INTEGRAL PART OF THAI CUISINE. IN THIS RECIPE, MINT IS ADDED TO FRESH GREENS AND TOPPED WITH GRILLED SIRLOIN FOR A TERRIFIC SALAD.

MARINADE:

One 1-inch piece fresh ginger, peeled and chopped

2 shallots, chopped

1 jalapeño pepper, seeded and chopped

2 tablespoons fresh lime juice

1 tablespoon fish sauce (nam pla)

1 tablespoon safflower oil

2$\frac{1}{2}$ to 3 pounds boneless sirloin steak, about $\frac{1}{2}$ inch thick

VINAIGRETTE:

2 tablespoons fresh lime juice

1 teaspoon light soy sauce

1 teaspoon fish sauce (nam pla)

1 teaspoon sugar

$\frac{1}{3}$ cup safflower oil

6 cups mixed salad greens

$\frac{1}{2}$ cup chopped fresh mint

2 scallions, trimmed and minced, for garnish

$\frac{1}{3}$ cup chopped peanuts, for garnish

1. Put the ginger, shallots, and pepper in a food processor and pulse to form a coarse paste, about 1 minute. Add 2 tablespoons lime juice, 1 tablespoon fish sauce, and 1 tablespoon safflower oil and pulse to combine. Put the steak on a large sheet of aluminum foil and coat both sides with the marinade. Wrap the steak in the foil and let stand, at room temperature, for 1 hour.

2. Prepare a gas or charcoal grill. When it's medium-hot (coals are covered with a light coating of ash and glow deep red), grill the steak, 4 to 5 minutes per side, for medium-rare, or until desired doneness. Let the steak rest for 10 minutes. Cut across the grain into $\frac{1}{4}$-inch slices.

3. In a small bowl, whisk together 2 tablespoons lime juice, soy sauce, 1 teaspoon fish sauce, and sugar to combine. Slowly add $\frac{1}{3}$ cup safflower oil, whisking constantly, until well combined.

4. Put the greens and mint in a large bowl and toss well to combine. Arrange on a large platter. Put the steak slices and their juices over the greens. Top the steak with the vinaigrette, garnish with the scallions and peanuts, and serve at once.

Serves 6

Grilled Sirloin Steak Salad
with Tomatoes, Basil & Capers

THIS BIG HEARTY SALAD HAS GOT IT ALL—RIPE TOMATOES, CAPERS, OLIVES, AND JUICY SIRLOIN STEAK HOT OFF THE GRILL. IF YOU'RE LUCKY ENOUGH TO HAVE LEFTOVERS, IT'S DELICIOUS TO EAT COLD THE NEXT DAY.

2 large ripe tomatoes,
   cut into 1-inch pieces

1/2 red onion, minced

2 tablespoons balsamic vinegar

5 tablespoons extra-virgin
   olive oil

1/4 cup fresh basil leaves,
   thinly sliced

Kosher salt and freshly ground
   black pepper

2 1/2 to 3 pounds boneless
   sirloin steak, about 1 inch
   thick

3 cloves garlic, thinly sliced

2 tablespoons drained capers

1/4 cup Niçoise olives, pitted
   and halved

2 tablespoons fresh lemon juice

6 cups mixed salad greens

1. Put the tomatoes, onion, 1 tablespoon of the vinegar, 2 tablespoons of the olive oil, basil, and salt and pepper to taste in a large bowl. Toss well to combine and let marinate, at room temperature, for 1/2 hour.

2. Prepare a gas or charcoal grill. When it's medium-hot (coals are covered with a light coating of ash and glow deep red), grill the steak for 5 to 7 minutes per side, for medium-rare, or until desired doneness. Let the steak rest for 10 minutes. Cut across the grain into 1/4-inch slices.

3. Heat the remaining 3 tablespoons olive oil in a skillet or sauté pan over medium heat. Add the garlic, capers, olives, lemon juice, and the remaining 1 tablespoon vinegar and simmer, stirring frequently, to blend the flavors, about 5 minutes. Toss together with the salad greens and set aside.

4. Arrange the greens on a large platter or individual plates. Put the steak slices and their juices over the greens. Top the steak with the tomato mixture and serve at once.

Serves 6

Grilled Lamb, Eggplant & Pepper Salad

SERVE THIS MEDITERRANEAN-STYLE SALAD WITH WARM PITA BREAD, HUMMUS, OLIVES, AND WINE FOR A DELIGHTFUL AL FRESCO LUNCH WITH FRIENDS. PERFECT FOR A SUNNY AFTERNOON.

MARINADE:

3 cloves garlic, thinly sliced

1 cup dry red wine

$1/4$ cup olive oil

$1/4$ cup chopped fresh mint

$1/4$ cup chopped fresh flat-leaf parsley

One $2^1/2$- to 3-pound butterflied leg of lamb

Kosher salt and freshly ground black pepper

1 eggplant, peeled and cut lengthwise into $1/2$-inch slices

2 red bell peppers, seeded, deveined, and quartered

2 yellow bell peppers, seeded, deveined, and quartered

4 cups mixed salad greens

1 tablespoon balsamic vinegar

1 tablespoon extra-virgin olive oil

1. In a medium bowl, whisk together the garlic, wine, $1/4$ cup olive oil, mint, and parsley. Put the lamb in a large nonreactive baking dish and sprinkle liberally with salt and pepper. Pour the marinade over the lamb, cover, and let marinate in the refrigerator for up to 6 hours or overnight, turning occasionally.

2. Put the eggplant slices and bell pepper quarters on a baking sheet. Brush them with olive oil and sprinkle with salt and pepper to taste.

3. Prepare a gas or charcoal grill. When it's medium-hot (coals are covered with a light coating of ash and glow deep red), grill the eggplant and peppers until tender and nicely charred, about 8 minutes. Cover and keep warm in the oven. Grill the lamb for 10 minutes per side, for medium-rare, or until desired doneness. Let the lamb rest for 10 minutes. Cut into thin slices on the diagonal. Cut the eggplant and peppers into 2-inch-long pieces.

4. Arrange the greens on a large platter. Alternating the pieces, arrange the lamb, eggplant, and pepper pieces on the greens. Whisk together the vinegar and extra-virgin olive oil and drizzle over the salad. Serve at once.

Serves 6

VINAIGRETTES
& DRESSINGS

Good vinaigrettes and dressings are all-important to great-tasting salads. Making flavorful vinaigrette is all about using the best-quality extra-virgin olive oil and vinegar you can find. Using top-quality ingredients is also the key to making delicious and creamy mayonnaise- or yogurt-based dressings.

Making vinaigrette and dressing from scratch is a snap, once you get the hang of it. Just keep in mind that balance is the key and no single ingredient should out-weigh or overpower the others.

Basic Vinaigrette

THIS IS THE BASIC MIXTURE OF OIL AND VINEGAR FOR ANY GREEN SALAD.

2 tablespoons red wine vinegar

5 tablespoons extra-virgin olive oil

Kosher salt and freshly ground
   black pepper

In a small bowl, whisk together the vinegar and olive oil until well combined. Season to taste with salt and pepper and whisk again.

Makes about $1/2$ cup

French Vinaigrette

THIS IS A GOOD RECIPE FOR A SALAD OF MIXED GREENS, ROMAINE LETTUCE, OR ENDIVE.
IT IS ALSO VERY TASTY DRIZZLED OVER ROASTED VEGETABLES.

2 tablespoons white wine vinegar

1 teaspoon Dijon mustard

2 teaspoons minced shallot

6 tablespoons extra-virgin olive oil

Kosher salt and freshly ground
   black pepper

In a small bowl, whisk together the vinegar, mustard, and shallot until well combined. Slowly add the olive oil and whisk until well combined. Season to taste with salt and pepper and whisk again.

Makes about $1/2$ cup

Garlic Vinaigrette

THIS IS A GOOD ALL-PURPOSE VINAIGRETTE FOR GARLIC LOVERS.

3 cloves garlic, finely minced

1 tablespoon Dijon mustard

2 tablespoons red wine vinegar

6 tablespoons extra-virgin olive oil

Kosher salt and freshly ground
   black pepper

In a small bowl, whisk together the garlic, mustard, and vinegar until well combined. Slowly add the olive oil and whisk until well combined. Season to taste with salt and pepper and whisk again.

Makes about 1/2 cup

Whole-Grain Mustard Vinaigrette

THIS IS A VERY GOOD DRESSING TO ADD TO POTATO SALAD. BE SURE TO MIX IT IN WHILE THE POTATOES ARE STILL WARM.

1 tablespoon whole-grain
   mustard

2 tablespoons balsamic vinegar

6 tablespoons extra-virgin olive oil

Kosher salt and freshly ground
   black pepper

In a small bowl, whisk together the mustard and vinegar until well combined. Slowly add the olive oil and whisk until well combined. Season to taste with salt and pepper and whisk again.

Makes about 1/2 cup

OILS

OLIVE OIL: Selecting olive oil can be confusing because of the different grades, colors, and flavors available. The best olive oils for salads are cold-pressed, a process that produces a natural low level of acidity. Extra-virgin olive oil is the cold-pressed result of the very first pressing of olives. Since it contains less than 1 percent acid, it is the fruitiest and most flavorful of olive oils and is therefore the best choice for making vinaigrette.

NUT OIL: Strong, aromatic oils such as walnut and hazelnut are good to combine with other oils for nutty-tasting vinaigrettes. They are also very good to use as a finishing touch on a salad. Mild lettuces topped with cheese and toasted nuts benefit from a drizzle of walnut or hazelnut oil just before serving.

VINEGARS

RED WINE VINEGAR: Versatile vinegar made from fermented red wine. Good in vinaigrettes accompanying strong-tasting greens.

WHITE WINE AND CHAMPAGNE VINEGARS: Pungent vinegars made from fermented white wine or champagne. Good in all types of vinaigrettes, especially ones made with citrus juices.

BALSAMIC VINEGAR: Intense, syrupy vinegar with a sweet-tart flavor. True balsamic vinegar is made in Italy from white Trebbiano grapes and is aged in barrels from a variety of woods. Excellent with all types of greens and vegetables. Also used for drizzling over peaches, berries, and melons.

RICE VINEGAR: Mellow, slightly sweet-tasting white vinegar that is made in Asia. Very good with salads of fish and shellfish.

Walnut Vinaigrette

THIS IS DELICIOUS WITH ANY COMBINATION OF MIXED GREENS AS WELL AS AN ENDIVE, ROASTED BEET, AND WALNUT SALAD.

1 teaspoon Dijon mustard

2 tablespoons white wine
vinegar

¼ cup walnut oil

1 tablespoon extra-virgin
olive oil

Kosher salt and freshly ground
black pepper

In a small bowl, whisk together the mustard and vinegar until well combined. Slowly add the oils and whisk until well combined. Season to taste with salt and pepper and whisk again.

Makes about ½ cup

Asian-Style Vinaigrette

THIS IS VERY GOOD TO SERVE WITH A CHINESE CABBAGE SALAD OR TO DRIZZLE OVER STEAMED ASPARAGUS OR BROCCOLI.

2 tablespoons rice wine vinegar

2 tablespoons light soy sauce

1 tablespoon minced fresh
ginger

6 tablespoons toasted
sesame oil

In a small bowl, whisk together the vinegar, soy sauce, and ginger until well combined. Slowly add the sesame oil and whisk until well combined.

Makes about ½ cup

Homemade Mayonnaise

SOME PEOPLE SHY AWAY FROM MAKING MAYONNAISE, BUT IT IS REALLY QUITE EASY TO MAKE AND THE
RESULTS ARE WELL WORTH THE EFFORT. THIS RECIPE IS THE BASE FOR ALL KINDS OF HOMEMADE SALAD
DRESSINGS (SEE PAGE 138).

2 egg yolks

1 teaspoon Dijon mustard

1 teaspoon fresh lemon juice

Pinch of kosher salt

½ cup safflower oil

½ cup olive oil

1. In a medium bowl or a food processor, whisk or process the egg yolks until thickened a bit. Add the mustard, lemon juice, and salt to taste and whisk or process until well blended.

2. Whisking constantly or with the machine running, slowly add the safflower oil, until incorporated. Slowly add the olive oil until the mixture is well incorporated and just beginning to turn stiff.

3. Add 1 tablespoon of hot water to thin the mixture. Add more hot water, if necessary, to achieve desired consistency. The mayonnaise will keep, covered, in the refrigerator for up to 1 week.

Makes about 1¼ cups

Buttermilk Dressing

BUTTERMILK ADDS A NICE TANGY FLAVOR TO THIS SIMPLE MAYONNAISE-BASED DRESSING. IT TASTES GREAT SPOONED OVER SUMMER-RIPE TOMATOES.

½ cup mayonnaise

1 tablespoon white vinegar

1 tablespoon fresh lemon juice

¼ cup buttermilk

2 tablespoons chopped
    red onion

2 tablespoons chopped
    fresh flat-leaf parsley

Kosher salt and freshly ground
    black pepper

In a small bowl, whisk together the mayonnaise, vinegar, and lemon juice. Add the buttermilk and whisk again. Stir in the onion and parsley. Season with salt and pepper to taste. The dressing will keep, covered, in the refrigerator for 1 day.

Makes about 1 cup

HOMEMADE MAYONNAISE DRESSING VARIATIONS

RUSSIAN DRESSING: Add chili sauce, cayenne pepper, and chopped onions and parsley.

THOUSAND ISLAND DRESSING: Add chili sauce and chopped hard-cooked egg, green pepper, and chives.

GREEN GODDESS DRESSING: Add fresh lemon juice and chopped watercress, scallions, tarragon, and parsley.

TARTAR SAUCE DRESSING: Add Dijon mustard, fresh lemon juice, chopped sweet or dill pickles, capers, shallots, and parsley.

Creamy Citrus Dressing

TRY THIS SUBTLY FLAVORED DRESSING WITH A SPINACH AND RED ONION SALAD. JUST DELICIOUS!

½ cup dry white wine

½ cup orange juice

½ cup mayonnaise

Kosher salt and freshly ground black pepper

Put the wine and orange juice in a small saucepan and bring to a boil over high heat. Reduce the heat and simmer until the liquid has been reduced to about ¼ cup, about 20 minutes. Remove from the heat and let cool to room temperature. Add the mayonnaise and blend well. Season to taste with salt and pepper. The dressing will keep, covered, in the refrigerator for 1 day.

Makes about ¾ cup

Yogurt-Dill Dressing

THIS DRESSING IS VERY GOOD TO SERVE WITH A COLD POACHED SALMON OR SMOKED TROUT SALAD.

3 cloves garlic, sliced

½ cup low-fat plain yogurt

1 tablespoon whole-grain mustard

1 tablespoon fresh lemon juice

¼ cup chopped fresh dill

2 tablespoons chopped fresh flat-leaf parsley

2 tablespoons extra-virgin olive oil

Kosher salt and freshly ground black pepper

In a blender or food processor, combine the garlic, yogurt, mustard, lemon juice, dill, and parsley and process until well blended. With the machine still running, add the olive oil and blend or process until well incorporated. Season to taste with salt and pepper. The dressing will keep, covered, in the refrigerator for 1 day.

Makes about ¾ cup

index